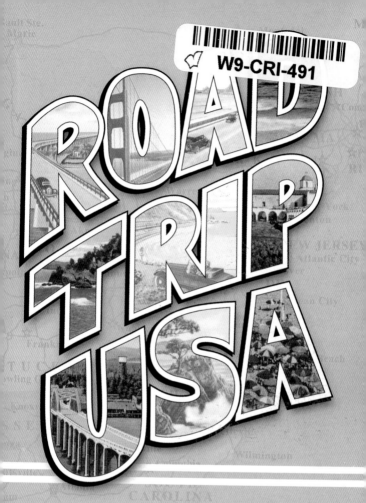

ROAD TRIP USA

Pacific Coast Highway

JAMIE JENSEN

AVALON
TRAVEL

Contents

WASHINGTON 8

Port Townsend 9
Sequim and Dungeness 11
Seattle 12
Port Angeles 14
Hurricane Ridge 16
Lake Crescent 17
Hwy-112: Strait of Juan de Fuca . .18
Neah Bay and Cape Flattery 18
Forks 19
Hoh Rainforest 20
Kalaloch and the Pacific Beaches . .21
Lake Quinault 22
Grays Harbor:
    Hoquiam and Aberdeen 23
Hwy-105: Westport and Tokeland .24
Willapa Bay: Raymond and
    South Bend 25
Long Beach Peninsula 25
Cape Disappointment 27

OREGON 28

Astoria 29
Fort Clatsop 30
Gearhart 31
Seaside 31
Portland 32
Ecola State Park 34
Cannon Beach 35
Neahkahnie Mountain
    and Oswald West State Park . .36
Tillamook .36
Three Capes Loop 37
Lincoln City 38
Depoe Bay 39
Cape Foulweather and the
    Devil's Punchbowl 39
Newport 40
Waldport .41
Yachats 42
Cape Perpetua 42
Heceta Head and the
    Sea Lion Caves 43
Florence 43

"Dune Country": Oregon's Sahara . .44
Coos Bay 45
Shore Acres State Park 45
Bandon 46
Port Orford and
    Humbug Mountain 47
Prehistoric Gardens 48
Gold Beach 48
Samuel H. Boardman State
    Scenic Corridor 49
Brookings: Harris Beach
    State Park 50

CALIFORNIA 50

Jedediah Smith Redwoods
    State Park 51
Crescent City 52
Del Norte Coast Redwoods
    State Park 53
Trees of Mystery and Klamath . . .53
Prairie Creek Redwoods
    State Park 54
Redwood National Park 54
Patrick's Point State Park 55
Arcata 56
Eureka 57
Samoa 59
Ferndale 60
The Lost Coast 61
Scotia 62
Humboldt Redwoods State Park . .62
Garberville and Redway 64
Leggett: The Chandelier
    Drive-Thru Tree 64
Rockport and Westport 66
Fort Bragg .66
Mendocino 68
Van Damme State Park 69
Anderson Valley   69
Elk 70
Point Arena and Gualala 71
Sea Ranch .71
Salt Point State Park 72
Fort Ross State Historic Park 72

Jenner, Guerneville, and the
    Russian River 73
Sonoma Coast State Park 74
Bodega Bay 74
Valley Ford 75
Point Reyes 75
Bolinas and Stinson Beach 76
Mt. Tamalpais, Muir Woods, and
    Muir Beach 77
Marin Headlands 78
Across San Francisco 79
San Francisco   80
Montara and Princeton 82
Half Moon Bay 82
Pescadero and Pigeon Point
    Lighthouse 83
Año Nuevo State Reserve 84
Big Basin Redwoods State Park . 85
Santa Cruz 85
Santa Cruz Beach Boardwalk . . . 87
Mystery Spot 88
Watsonville, Castroville,
    and Moss Landing 88
San Juan Bautista 89
Monterey 90
Pacific Grove 92
The 17-Mile Drive and
    Pebble Beach 94
Carmel 95
Point Lobos State
    Natural Reserve 98
Garrapata State Park 98
Andrew Molera State Park 99
Big Sur Village 99
Pfeiffer Big Sur State Park 100
Pfeiffer Beach 100
Ventana Inn & Spa and the
    Post Ranch Inn 101
Nepenthe 102
Julia Pfeiffer Burns State Park . 103
Esalen and Lucia 103
Nacimiento-Fergusson Road and
    Mission San Antonio de Padua . 104
San Simeon: Hearst Castle 104

Cambria 106
Cayucos 107
Morro Bay 107
San Luis Obispo 108
Pismo Beach 112
Guadalupe and Santa Maria . . . 113
Lompoc and
    La Purisima Mission 113
Buellton and Solvang 114
Gaviota State Park
    and Refugio State Beach 115
Santa Barbara 115
Channel Islands National Park . 118
Ventura 118
Simi Valley 119
Pacific Coast Highway Beaches . 120
Malibu 121
Topanga and the Getty Villa . . . 122
Crossing Los Angeles 123
Los Angeles 124
Long Beach 126
Huntington Beach 127
Anaheim: Disneyland Resort . . . 127
Richard Nixon
    Presidential Library 129
Newport Beach 129
Crystal Cove State Park 130
Laguna Beach 131
San Juan Capistrano 132
San Clemente 133
Old Mission San Luis Rey
    de Francia 133
Oceanside 134
Carlsbad:
    La Costa and Legoland 135
San Diego 136
Del Mar and Torrey Pines
    State Natural Reserve 138
La Jolla 139
Driving San Diego 139

INDEX 140

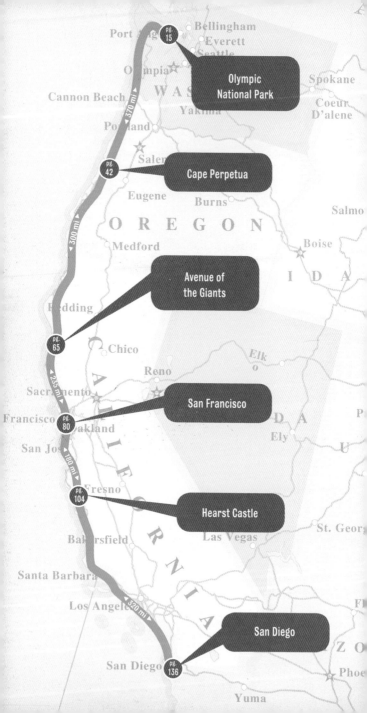

Port A__ ○ Bellingham
○ Everett
○ Seattle

pg. 15

Olympic National Park

Olympia ☆

Cannon Beach

WAS__

Spokane

Yakima

Coeur D'alene

Portland ○

▲ 370 mi ▲

Salem ☆

pg. 42

Cape Perpetua

Eugene ○

Burns

Salmo

O R E G O N

Medford ○

Boise ☆

I D A

▲ 300 mi ▲

Avenue of the Giants

Redding ○

pg. 65

Chico ○

Elk o ○

C_____

Reno ☆

San Francisco

▲ 235 mi ▲

Sacramento ☆

D A

Francisco ○

pg. 80

Oakland

Ely ○

San Jos__

▲ 180 mi ▲

pg. 104

○ Fresno

Hearst Castle

St. Georg__

Bakersfield ○

Las Vegas

Santa Barbara

N

I

A

Los Angeles ▲ 320 mi ▲

F__

San Diego

pg. 136

San Diego ○

Z O

☆ Phoe__

Yuma ○

Pacific Coast Highway

CALIFORNIA 1

The amazing thing about the West Coast is that it is still mostly wild, open, and astoundingly beautiful country, where you can drive for miles and miles and have the scenery all to yourself.

Between Olympic National Park and San Diego, California

4400   PALACE OF BETTER HOUSING AND HOUSE OF HOSPITALITY FROM LAGOON

AMERICA'S EXPOSITION AT SAN DIEGO, CALIFORNIA

For some reason, when people elsewhere in the country refer to the Pacific Coast, particularly **California**, it's apparent that they think it's a land of kooks and crazies, an overbuilt suburban desert supporting only shopping malls, freeways, and body-obsessed airheads. All this may be true in small pockets, but the amazing thing about the Pacific Coast—from the dense green forests of western **Washington** to the gorgeous beaches of Southern California—is that it is still mostly wild, open, and astoundingly beautiful country, where you can drive for miles and miles and have the scenery all to yourself.

Starting at the northwest tip of the United States at **Olympic National Park,** and remaining within sight of the ocean almost all the way south to the Mexican border, this 1,650-mile, mostly two-lane route takes in everything from temperate rainforest to near-desert. Most of the Pacific Coast is in the public domain, accessible, and protected from development within national, state, and local parks, which provide habitat for such rare creatures as mountain lions, condors, and gray whales.

Heading south, after the rough-and-tumble logging and fishing communities of Washington State, you cross the mouth of the Columbia River and follow the comparatively peaceful and quiet **Oregon** coastline, where recreation has by and large replaced industry, and where dozens of quaint and not-so-quaint communities line the ever-changing shoreline. At the midway point, you pass through the great redwood forests of Northern California, where the tallest and most majestic living things on earth line the "Avenue of the Giants," home also to some of the best (meaning gloriously kitsch) remnants of the golden age of car-borne tourism: drive-through trees, drive-on trees, houses carved out of trees, and much more. The phenomenally beautiful coastline of Northern California is rivaled only by the incredible coast of **Big Sur** farther south, beyond which stretch the beachfronts of Southern California. The land of palm trees, beach boys, and surfer girls of popular lore really does exist, though only in the southernmost quarter of the state.

Along with the overwhelming scale of its natural beauty, the West Coast is remarkable for the abundance of well-preserved historic sites—most of which haven't been torn down, built on, or even built around—that stand as vivid evocations of life on what was once the most distant frontier of the New World. While rarely as old as places on the East Coast, or as impressive as those in Europe, West Coast sites are quite diverse and include the Spanish colonial missions of California, Russian and English fur-trading outposts, and the place where Lewis and Clark first sighted the Pacific after their long slog across the continent.

Last but certainly not least are the energizing cities—**Seattle** and **Portland** in the north, **San Francisco** in the middle, and **Los Angeles** and **San Diego** to the south—which serve as gateways to (or civilized respites from) the landscapes in between them. Add to these the dozens of small and not-so-small towns along the coast, with alternating blue-collar ports and upscale vacation retreats, and you have a great range of food, drink, and accommodation options. Local cafés, seafood grills, and bijou restaurants abound, as do places to stay—from youth hostels in old lighthouses to roadside motels (including the world's first, which still stands in lovely San Luis Obispo, California) to homespun B&B inns in old farmhouses.

Big Sur

WASHINGTON

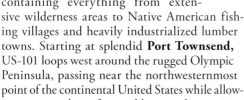

The coast of Washington is a virtual microcosm of the Pacific Northwest, containing everything from extensive wilderness areas to Native American fishing villages and heavily industrialized lumber towns. Starting at splendid **Port Townsend,** US-101 loops west around the rugged Olympic Peninsula, passing near the northwesternmost point of the continental United States while allowing access to the unforgettable natural attractions—sandy, driftwood-strewn beaches; primeval old-growth forests; and pristine mountain lakes and glaciated alpine peaks, to name just a few—of **Olympic National Park.** The roadside landscape varies from dense woods to clear-cut tracts of recently harvested timber, with innumerable rivers and streams perhaps the most obvious signs of the immense amount of rainfall (about 12 feet) the region receives every year. Scattered towns, from **Port Angeles** in the north to the twin cities of **Grays Harbor** on the coast, are staunchly blue-collar communities almost wholly dependent upon natural resources—not only trees, but also salmon, oysters, and other seafood. Though the tourism trade has been increasing steadily, visitor services are still few and far between, so plan ahead.

Though it's not on the ocean, the Puget Sound port city of **Seattle** makes a good starting or finishing point to this Pacific Coast road trip.

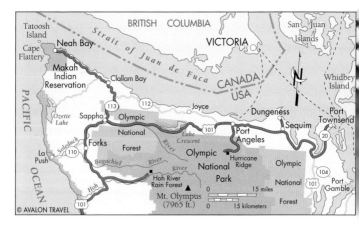

Port Townsend

Few places in the world can match the concentration of natural beauty or the wealth of architecture found in tiny **Port Townsend** (pop. 9,113). One of the oldest towns in Washington, Port Townsend was laid out in 1852 and reached a peak of activity in the 1880s. But after the railroads focused on Seattle and Puget Sound as their western terminus, the town sat quietly for most of the next century until the 1960s, when an influx of arts-oriented refugees took over the waterfront warehouses and cliff-top mansions, converting them to galleries, restaurants, and comfy B&Bs while preserving the town's turn-of-the-20th-century character.

Port Townsend is neatly divided into two halves: Multi-story brick warehouses and commercial buildings line Water Street and the wharves along the bay, while lovely old Victorian houses cover the bluffs above. It's basically a great place to wander, but there are a couple of sights worth seeing, particularly the landmark **City Hall** (250 Madison St.) along the east end of Water Street. Half of this eclectic gothic pile now houses a local historical museum with three floors of odds and ends tracing Port Townsend history, including the

Fort Worden, on the north side of Port Townsend, is a retired military base that served as a location for the Richard Gere movie *An Officer and a Gentleman.* Now home to a wonderful natural history museum, the old fort also hosts an excellent series of annual music and arts festivals; contact the Centrum at 360/385-3102 for schedules and more information.

Toward Seattle: Port Gamble

You have a number of options if traveling to or from Port Townsend. You can follow US-101 around the western Olympic Peninsula, or take a ferry via Whidbey Island and explore it and the even prettier San Juan Islands to the north. Last, but not least, you can take a middle route across the Kitsap Peninsula, then catch a ferry to Seattle (see pages 12–13).

This last route, which includes a trip on the very frequent Washington State Ferries between Kingston and Edmonds, has the great advantage of taking you through the lovely old logging town of **Port Gamble,** a slice of New England on the shores of Puget Sound. The entire town is a historic district, with dozens of immaculate Victorian buildings standing along maple tree—lined streets. After wandering past the saltbox houses, have a look inside the large Port Gamble General Store, which includes a seashell museum and a café, or visit the photo-filled **Port Gamble Historic Museum** ($4; 360/297-8078) below the store.

old city jail where Jack London spent a night on his way to the Klondike goldfields in 1897.

Not surprisingly, considering the extensive tourist trade, Port Townsend has a number of good restaurants and bars. You'll find many of the best places at the east end of town near the corner of Water and Quincy Streets. For breakfast, try the **Salal Cafe** (634 Water St.; 360/385-6532). For lunch or dinner, one of the best seafood places is the **Silverwater Cafe** (237 Taylor St.; 360/385-6448), near the Quincy Street dock. The old waterfront neighborhood also holds a pair of hotels in restored 1880s buildings: **The Waterstreet Hotel** ($50 and up; 635 Water St.; 360/385-5467 or 800/735-9810) and the quieter **The Palace Hotel** ($59 and up; 1004 Water St.; 360/385-0773), where the room names play up the building's past use as a brothel.

The most comfortable accommodations in Port Townsend are the many 1880s-era B&Bs dotting the bluffs above the port area, including the ever-popular **The Old Consulate Inn** ($99 and up; 313 Walker St.; 360/385-6753), where some of the plush rooms come with a view of the Olympic Mountains and all come with a hearty multi-course breakfast. For less-pricey lodging, there's a **campground** (360/344-4400) and the **HI-Olympic Guesthouse & Hostel** ($28 per person; 360/385-0655), with dorm beds in the old Army barracks at Fort Worden, on the coast two miles north of town.

Sequim and Dungeness

Forty minutes southwest of Port Townsend via Hwy-20 and US-101, **Sequim** (pop. 6,606; pronounced "SKWIM") sits in the rain shadow of the Olympic Mountains and so tends to be much drier and sunnier than spots even a few miles west. Though it retains its rural feel, Sequim's historic farming-and-fishing economy is quickly switching over to tourism, with tracts of new homes filling up the rolling, waterfront landscape and a new freeway bypassing the center of town. It's ideal cycling country, for the moment at least, with acres and acres of lavender farms lining quiet country roads.

Sequim lavender fields

Coming in from the east on two-lane US-101, the first thing you pass is the large, modern John Wayne Marina, built on land donated by The Duke's family. The US-101 frontage through town is lined by the usual franchised fast-food outlets and some unique variations, like the 1950s-themed **Hi-Way 101 Diner** (392 W. Washington St.; 360/683-3388), in the heart of town.

Just north of US-101, the **Museum & Arts Center in the Sequim-Dungeness Valley** (10 am–4 pm Tues.–Sun., except the last Sun. of every month; donation; 175 W. Cedar St.; 360/683-8110) houses everything from 12,000-year-old mastodon bones discovered on a nearby farm to exhibits of Native American

The natural cut of the **Hood Canal** on the east side of the Olympic Peninsula is one of the West Coast's prime oyster-growing estuaries, source of the gourmet Quilcenes, Hama Hamas, and other varieties available at roadside stands, shops, and restaurants throughout the region.

Sequim's annual **Irrigation Festival,** held every May, is Washington's oldest continuing community celebration. The **Lavender Festival,** in July, is also very popular.

The Native American–owned **7 Cedars Casino** stands above US-101 at the foot of Sequim Bay, fronted by totem poles.

Seattle

An engaging and energetic combination of scenic beauty, blue-collar grit, and high-tech panache has made Seattle one of the most popular cities in the United States, for visitors and residents alike. A young city, historically and demographically, Seattle has managed to preserve much of its heavy industrial heritage as parks and museums, if not as economic engines. The eco-conscious, civic-minded city spreads over a series of hills, surrounded by the waters of Puget Sound (be sure to ride a ferry or two!), with a backdrop of the snow-capped Cascade and Olympic Mountains. The evergreen Seattle can be an entrancing city—at least when the sun comes out, which no matter what people say is likely to happen at least once during your stay.

The heart of downtown Seattle, **Pike Place Market** is a raucous fish, crafts, and farmers market with some 250 different stalls and stores

Pike Place Market

filling a 1930s municipal-feeling building that steps along the waterfront. For a respite from the hubbub, head two blocks south to the postmodern **Seattle Art Museum,** 1300 1st Avenue (closed Mon.; $13; 206/654-3100), and enjoy the amazing collection of regional Native American art and artifacts on display. Downtown's other piece of noteworthy recent architecture is the shiny **Seattle Central Library** at 1000 4th Avenue, a fantastic (and free!) high-tech (some say hermetic) space whose multifaceted glass diamond exterior steps down between two city blocks.

At the south edge of downtown, a half mile from the Pike Place Market, the 30-block Pioneer Square historic district preserves the original core of the city, which boomed in the late 1890s with the Klondike Gold Rush. Another essential place to go is the **Seattle Center** (206/684-8582), north of downtown at Broad Street and 5th Avenue North, built for the 1962 World's Fair. Take the elevator to the top of the landmark Space Needle or ride the monorail, or Windstorm roller coaster, bumper cars, or a dozen other funfair attractions at the summer-only Fun Forest (noon–midnight; pay-per-ride). The Seattle Center, location for Seattle's excellent annual Labor Day arts and music festival, Bumbershoot, is also home to the intriguing **Experience Music Project** (206/367-5483), a hands-on musical exploration and living memorial to the city's native-born guitar genius,

Jimi Hendrix. A don't-miss photo opportunity: A statue of Chief Seattle with the Space Needle rising behind him.

Besides funding the Experience Music Project, Microsoft millionaire Paul Allen has indulged his taste for Space Age adventure by subsidizing the private rocketship SpaceShipOne, and closer to home by renovating the world's last intact **Cinerama Theatre** (206/441-3080), an early 1960s icon at 2100 Fourth Avenue.

Spectators enjoy downtown views and Puget Sound sunsets at SAFECO Field ballpark, south of Pioneer Square, where the **Seattle Mariners** (206/346-4001) play.

Practicalities

Seattle's main airport is Seattle–Tacoma International ("Sea-Tac"), a half-hour drive south of downtown Seattle via the I-5 freeway. Seattle's freeways are often filled to capacity most of the day, but the best drive-through tour of Seattle follows old US-99 along the Alaska Way Viaduct, a concrete freeway that cuts along the downtown waterfront, runs through a tunnel, then follows Aurora Avenue on a soaring bridge over the Lake Union Canal. (By the way, under the Aurora Bridge sits one of Seattle's biggest pieces of auto-art: the Aurora Troll, caught in the act of eating an old VW Beetle.)

Most everything of visitor interest in Seattle is within the walkably compact downtown, where an extensive bus system runs in a fare-free zone; there's also a mile-long monorail ($1), linking 5th and Pine Streets downtown with the Seattle Center and Space Needle.

The niftiest place to stay is the **Hotel Andra** ($180 and up; 206/448-8600), at 2000 4th Avenue, a fully modernized 1920s hotel three blocks from Pike Place Market. The cheapest place to stay has to be the **HI-Seattle Hostel** (206/622-5443) at 84 Union Street, which offers clean and comfortable dorm beds for around $25, right along the waterfront next to Pike Place Market.

Seafood, not surprisingly, is the thing Seattle restaurants do best, and the city is full of great places to eat fish (the sushi here is as good as it gets, outside Japan). For fish-and-chips or cheap, fresh oysters (and Washington produces more oysters than anywhere else in the United States), head down to **Emmett Watson's Oyster Bar** (206/448-7721) at the north end of Pike Place Market. More down-home fare is served up for breakfast, lunch, and dinner at the **5 Spot** (206/285-7768), at 1502 Queen Anne Avenue in the residential Queen Anne district, a mile northwest of downtown high above Lake Union.

The best source of advance information on visiting Seattle is the Seattle Convention and Visitors Bureau (206/461-5840).

cultures and pioneer farm implements. From the museum, a well-marked road winds north for seven miles before reaching the waterfront again at **Dungeness,** where a 5.5-mile-long sand spit, the country's longest, protects a shellfish-rich wildlife refuge. All that remains of the abandoned fishing community that existed here through the 1890s is an old schoolhouse and the hit-or-miss local landmark **The 3 Crabs** (360/683-4264), overlooking Dungeness Harbor, which has been serving up fresh fish and local Dungeness crab for over 45 years.

Stay in Sequim at **Groveland Cottage Bed and Breakfast** ($110 and up; 4861 Sequim-Dungeness Way; 360/683-3565), a quaint B&B just a half mile from the harbor, or at the popular waterfront **Juan de Fuca Cottages** ($120 and up; 182 Marine Dr.; 866/683-4433), 2.5 miles to the west.

Port Angeles

A busy, industrial city at the center of the northern Olympic Peninsula, **Port Angeles** (pop. 19,038) makes a handy base for visiting the nearby wilderness of Olympic National Park. The town is slowly but surely recovering from its traditional dependence on logging, and the waterfront, which once hummed to the sound of lumber and pulp mills, is now bustling with tour-

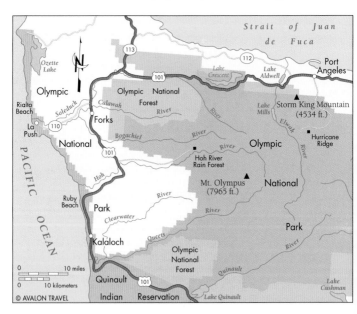

Olympic National Park

Olympic National Park, in the heart of the Olympic Peninsula, is a diversely beautiful corner of the country, combining features of Maine's rocky coast and the snowcapped peaks of the Rocky Mountains with the unique rainforests covering the park's Pacific coastal valleys. The rugged, nearly million-acre landscape, ranging from rocky shores to impassably dense forests, resisted exploitation and development until the turn of the 20th century, when local conservationists persuaded Teddy Roosevelt to declare much of the peninsula a national monument, a movement that eventually resulted in the establishment of Olympic National Park in 1938.

There are no roads and few trails across the peninsula, so you have to choose your points of entry depending upon what you want to see. The different areas of Olympic National Park are covered in the surrounding pages, but the most popular part of the park is Hurricane Ridge, which rises high above Port Angeles and offers great views of the silvery peaks and the many glaciers that flank them. (The wildflowers can be spectacular in late spring.)

At the northwestern corner of the park, Lake Crescent sits serenely amidst the forests and peaks, while on the western slopes, the temperate rainforests of the usually wet and rainy river valleys hold some of the world's largest trees, all draped with a thick fabric of mosses. At the western edge of the peninsula, the almost completely undeveloped Pacific Ocean coastline, added to the park in 1953, offers miles of sandy beaches and rocky headlands, littered only with driftwood logs and vibrant tidepools.

ists wandering along a 6.5-mile walking trail and enjoying the sealife (sea slugs, starfish, and octopuses) on display at the small but enjoyable **Feiro Marine Life Center** (daily during summer, weekends during off-season; $4), on the centrally located Port Angeles City Pier.

Malls, gas stations, and fast-food franchises line the US-101 frontage through town, but life in Port Angeles, for locals and visitors alike, centers on the attractive downtown area, two blocks inland from the waterfront around Lincoln Street and 1st Street. Here cafés like **First Street Haven** (107 E. 1st St.;

360/457-0352) offer great breakfasts and good yet inexpensive soup-and-salad lunches, while amiable bars and pubs like **Peaks,** around the corner (130 S. Lincoln Ave.; 360/452-2802), draw bikers, hikers, and loggers with their pub grub and good beers (more than 50 bottles, plus some intriguing "home brews"). If you're waiting for a boat, or are fresh off of one, more places to eat and drink surround the ferry terminal.

Weather on the Olympic Peninsula varies widely from place to place. The peaks and coastal valleys of Olympic National Park receive as much as 200 inches of rainfall each year, while the nearby town of Sequim garners an average of just 15–17 inches annually.

Places to stay in Port Angeles vary. You'll find highway motels, including the **Quality Inn Uptown** ($85 and up; 101 E. 2nd St.; 360/457-9434), and the **Red Lion** ($129 and up; 360/452-9215), on the water at the foot of Lincoln Street. There are also many characterful B&Bs, like the popular **Inn at Rooster Hill** ($99 and up; 360/452-4933).

Hurricane Ridge

High above Port Angeles, **Hurricane Ridge** provides the most popular access to Olympic National Park. A paved road twists and turns 17 miles up a steep 7 percent grade to the mile-high summit, where, on a clear day, you can gape at the breathtaking

Ferries to Victoria, British Columbia

From Port Angeles, the Black Ball Ferry Line carries cars and passengers (around $60 per car and driver one-way, plus $16.50 per additional person; 360/457-4491), shuttling across the water to and from pretty Victoria, the provincial capital of British Columbia, one of Canada's most popular destinations. Ships leave Port Angeles at the middle of the attractively landscaped waterfront and arrive very near the center of Victoria, making for a great day trip from either place. At the Port Angeles dock there's a very helpful information center packed with maps and brochures on Victoria and the rest of B.C., or you can call **Tourism Victoria** at 800/663-3883.

360-degree views of mountain, valley, and sea. A lodge at the crest provides food and drink, and a concession offers ski and snowshoe rentals on winter weekends. Trails lead down into the backcountry, where you're likely to spot marmots, deer, and bald eagles—and if you're lucky, maybe an elk or a mountain lion. From Hurricane Ridge, thrill-seeking drivers and mountain bikers may get a kick out of Obstruction Point Road, a twisting gravel road that continues (without guardrails!) for another eight miles along the crest from the parking lot. In winter, the snowed-in road becomes a popular cross-country skiing trail.

Apart from the area right around Hurricane Ridge, most of the Olympic National Park backcountry is fairly wet and rugged. If you plan to camp overnight, be prepared, and be sure to get a permit from the Olympic National Park **visitors center** (360/565-3130) in Port Angeles, just south of US-101 on the road up to Hurricane Ridge. This is also the best place to pick up general information on the rest of the park, which extends all the way west to the rainforest areas along the coastal valleys.

Lake Crescent

One of the most idyllic spots in the entire Pacific Northwest, the fjord-like **Lake Crescent,** over eight miles long and some 625 feet deep, lies right alongside two-lane US-101, just 18 miles west of Port Angeles. The placid surface reflects the clouds and surrounding peaks, including 4,537-foot Mount Storm King; to appreciate the tranquil beauty, rent a rowboat from the Lake Crescent Lodge and float around under your own steam. Starting from the lodge, a popular mile-long hike follows a well-maintained nature trail up to the delicate cascade of 90-foot **Marymere Falls,** while along the north shore an abandoned railroad grade is open to hikers and mountain bikers.

Incomparably situated along US-101 on the lake's southeast shore, **Lake Crescent Lodge** (open May–Oct. only, except for the Fireplace Cottages open on the weekends; $110 and up; 360/928-3211) was originally built in 1916 and has been hosting visitors ever since. Fairly rustic rooms are available in the old lodge, which also has a cozy dining room. Other accommodations are available in the adjacent cabins and motel, though the whole place is booked solid on summer weekends, so reserve as soon as you can. Another nice place to stay is the **Log Cabin Resort** ($121 and up; 360/928-3325), three miles north of US-101 on the "sunny northeast shore," with lodge rooms and waterfront A-frame cabins.

In the forested hills above US-101, **Sol Duc Hot Springs Resort** ($160 and up; 360/327-3583) has family-friendly cabins and a restaurant set around a swimming pool and natural hot spring ($12.25 for non-guests).

Hwy-112: Strait of Juan de Fuca

The Strait of Juan de Fuca, the narrow inlet that links the open Pacific with Puget Sound and divides the United States from Canada, was named for the Greek sailor (real name: Apostolos Valerianos) who first mapped it while working for the Spanish Crown in 1592. On a clear day, you can get some great views across the strait from Hwy-112, which runs along the shore from US-101 all the way to the tip of the Olympic Peninsula at Neah Bay. Though it looks like a great drive on the map, Hwy-112 is a very narrow and winding road with some surprisingly steep hills and thick woods that block much of the view, all of which (in addition to the plentiful logging trucks) can make it less than ideal for bicycling or even a scenic drive.

Along Hwy-112, you may pass a pair of fish-headed, human-legged, sneaker-wearing statues. Don't be alarmed.

Neah Bay and Cape Flattery

From the crossroads at **Sappho** on US-101, Hwy-113 leads north, linking up with Hwy-112 on a long and winding 40-mile detour through Clallam Bay to **Cape Flattery,** the northwesternmost tip of the continental United States. The highway is paved as far as the town of **Neah Bay,** a tiny (pop. 865) and somewhat bedraggled community that's the center of the Makah Indian Reservation. Salmon and halibut fishing, both by Makah and by visitors, is about the only activity here, though the tribe does have the impressive and modern **Makah Museum** (daily; $5; 360/645-2711), one of the best anthropological museums in the state. Most of the displays are of artifacts uncovered

Cape Flattery

in 1970, when a winter storm exposed the pristine remains of a 500-year-old coastal village that had been buried in a mudslide—the Pompeii of the Pacific Northwest. Other galleries display finely crafted baskets, a full-scale longhouse complete with recorded chants, and a whaling canoe from which fearless Makah harpooners would jump into the surf and sew up the jaws of dying whales, to keep them from sinking. If you want a special souvenir, the museum gift shop displays and sells a variety of high-quality arts and crafts made by Makah people.

In the late 1990s, as part of an effort to preserve tribal traditions and instill pride in younger Makah, the Makah tribe resumed small-scale hunting of migratory gray whales, which they had voluntarily ceased when the whales became endangered a century ago. Though the hunting was largely ceremonial, the news raised the hackles of wildlife organizations, which filed lawsuits and staged loud protests to prevent whales from being killed.

The Hwy-112/113 route twists along the rocky and wooded shore of the Strait of Juan de Fuca, but reaching the actual cape itself isn't difficult. From Neah Bay, the well-maintained western half of the Cape Loop Road winds along the Pacific to a parking area that gives access to a trail that brings you to the top of a cliff overlooking the crashing surf and offshore **Tatoosh Island.** On a sunny day it's a gorgeous vista, but if the weather's less than perfect (which it often is) your time would be much better spent inside the Makah Museum.

Forks

Bending southwest along the banks of the Sol Duc River, US-101 passes through miles of green forests under ever-gray skies to reach **Forks** (pop. 3,532), the commercial center of the northwestern Olympic Peninsula. Named for its location astride the Sol Duc and Bogachiel Rivers, Forks is a die-hard lumber town grappling with the inevitable change to more ecologi-

The old-growth forests of **Olympic National Park** provide prime habitat for the northern spotted owl, an endangered species whose preservation has sparked heated debate throughout the Pacific Northwest.

cally sustainable alternatives, mainly tourism. Visitors come to fish for steelhead during the late-summer runs, to beachcomb along the rugged coast, or to visit the remarkable rainforests of Olympic National Park. The main attractions in Forks these days are sights related to the wildly popular teenage vampire novels and films of *The Twilight Saga,* which were set here in Forks. Vampires aside, the main event is the quirky, summer-only **Forks Timber Museum** (Tues.–Sat.; 360/374-9663), on US-101 on the south edge of town, packed with handsaws, chainsaws, and other logging gear as well as antique cooking stoves and displays telling the town's characterful history. There's also a forest-fire lookout tower perched outside the upper floor gallery.

With three gas stations and five motels, Forks is not a metropolis by any stretch of the imagination, but it does offer the best range of services between Port Angeles and Aberdeen. **Sully's Burgers** (220 N. Forks Ave.) is a good burger stand on US-101 at the north end of town. There are also a couple of Chinese and Mexican places, plus salmon sandwiches at **The Smoke House Restaurant** and pretty good pies at **Pacific Pizza** (870 S. Forks Ave.). Stay at **The Forks Motel** ($60–160; 351 S. Forks Ave.; 360/374-6243) or a more peaceful B&B, the **Miller Tree Inn Bed and Breakfast** ($115 and up; 654 E. Division St.; 360/374-6806), about half a mile east of Forks's solitary stoplight.

South of Forks along US-101, **Bogachiel State Park** has over 100 forested acres of very nice campsites (with showers!) along the Bogachiel River. Sites are first-come, first-served, and cost around $10 for tents, $15 for RV hookups (360/374-6356).

For more information, contact the Forks **visitors center** (360/374-2531), next to the Timber Museum, which also serves as clearinghouse for *Twilight*-related tourism.

Hoh Rainforest

If you have time to visit only one of the lush rainforest areas of Washington's northwest coast, head for the **Hoh Rainforest,** 12 miles south of Forks and then 18 miles east along a well-signed and well-paved road. Not only is this the most easily accessible of these incredibly lush, old-growth areas, the Hoh Rainforest is also among the least disturbed, with a thick, wet blanket of vibrant green ferns, mosses, and lichens covering every inch

Ruby Beach

of the earth at the foot of massive hemlocks, cedars, and towering Sitka spruce. Displays inside the visitors center tell all about the forest's flora and fauna and how they are affected by the massive rainfall here— upwards of 140 inches every year. There's also a wheelchair-accessible nature trail and a wide range of hiking trails, including the quickest access to the icy summit of 7,965-foot Mt. Olympus, 22 miles away in the glacier-packed alpine highlands at the heart of the park.

The closest services to the Hoh Rainforest are in Forks, but budget travelers may want to take advantage of the $10-a-night bunks at the amiable **Rain Forest Hostel** (360/374-2270), 23 miles south of Forks along US-101 (between milemarkers 169 and 170), midway between the Hoh Rainforest and the coast at Ruby Beach.

If you're very lucky, you might spy one of the rare Roosevelt elk, whose protection was one of the reasons Olympic National Park was established; if you're unlucky, you might also come face-to-face with a mountain lion, which can be dangerous but generally avoids contact with humans.

Kalaloch and the Pacific Beaches

Looping around the northern Olympic Peninsula, US-101 finally reaches the coast 27 miles south of Forks at **Ruby Beach,** where wave-sculpted sea stacks frame a photogenic, driftwood-strewn cove. From Ruby Beach, US-101 runs south through the wild coastal section of Olympic National Park, which is almost always foggy and cool, even when the weather's sunny and hot just a mile inland. While almost the entire coast south from Cape Flattery is protected within the national park, this is the only easily accessible stretch. Parking areas along the highway, numbered from Beach 6 to Beach 1 north to south, give access to 20 miles of generally deserted beach, backed by rocky bluffs and packed with tidepools, driftwood castles, and an incredible variety of flotsam and jetsam.

At the southern end of this

© AVALON TRAVEL

short but sweet stretch of coastline, between Beach 2 and Beach 3, 25 miles north of Lake Quinault, **Kalaloch Lodge** ($134 and up; 360/962-2271) is a modern resort, with a coffee shop and a nice restaurant overlooking a picturesque cove. There's also a gas station, a summer-only **ranger station** across US-101, and an oceanside **campground** just to the north.

Lake Quinault

Spreading in a broad valley at the southwest corner of Olympic National Park, **Lake Quinault** offers lush rainforest groves within a short walk or drive of most creature comforts. The lake has served for decades as a popular resort destination—cabins, lodges,

From US-101 at **Hoquiam,** Hwy-109 runs west and north along the Pacific Ocean through a series of small fishing ports and beach resorts to the heavily logged lands of the Quinault Indian Reservation.

and stores dating from the 1920s line the southern shore, just outside the park boundary—and the old-growth forests here have survived intact, though the naked tracts of clear-cut timber along US-101 north and south of the lake give a good sense of what the area might have looked like had Teddy Roosevelt and friends not stepped in to protect it around the turn of the 20th century.

Before or after the hike, stop at the USFS **ranger station** (360/956-2400) on the south shore, where you can get details of the other excellent hikes in the Lake Quinault area and pick up a map of the guided driving tour around the lake, including the location of the many record-size trees. The roughly four-mile-long **Quinault Loop Trail** winds on a paved path from the ranger station along crashing Cascade Creek up through an old-growth rainforest of alders and bigleaf maples, whose leaves grow upwards of 12 inches across (and provide some splendid "fall color"). Midway along, the trail crosses a raised wooden boardwalk through a fecund cedar swamp, then drops down again along another creek before returning by way of the lakeshore.

On the lakeshore right next to the ranger station, historic **Lake Quinault Lodge** ($79 and up; 360/288-2900) is well worth a look, with a rustic but spacious lobby opening onto lakefront lawns, though the rooms could do with some TLC. The **Rain Forest Resort Village** ($75 and up; 360/288-2535), at the east end of the lake, besides offering comfortable and reasonably priced accommodations (from camping to cabins) and very good food in the Salmon House restaurant, also holds the **World's Largest Spruce Tree,** a 191-foot giant.

Grays Harbor: Hoquiam and Aberdeen

GRAYS HARBOR HISTORICAL SEAPORT

The Olympic Peninsula is cut off from the southern Washington coast by the spade-shaped bay of **Grays Harbor,** named for an early American sea captain and explorer, Robert Gray. Long the state's prime lumber port, Grays Harbor still processes huge piles of trees, but in many ways what's most interesting is the contrast between the two towns here, Hoquiam and Aberdeen.

At the western end of Grays Harbor, tidy **Hoquiam** (pop. 8,726; kind of rhymes with "requiem") celebrates its lumber-based history with an annual Loggers PlayDay bash, complete with ax-throwing and tree-climbing competitions, the second weekend in September. The rest of the year, get a feel for the bygone days of the lumber industry at **Hoquiam's Castle Bed & Breakfast** ($125 and up; 515 Chenault Ave.; 360/533-2005), on a hillside three blocks off US-101, a 20-room mansion built in 1897 by a local lumber baron. Another grand old timber-magnate mansion now houses **The Polson Museum** (Wed.–Sun; donation; 1611 Riverside Ave.; 360/533-5862), on US-101. Not surprisingly, it's devoted to local history, with information on logging.

East of Hoquiam along the Chehalis River at the head of Grays Harbor, **Aberdeen** (pop. 16,896) is much more heavily industrialized and thus has been even harder hit by the continuing downturn in the Northwest timber industry. The downtown area has more than a few rough edges, but it also holds one of the more high-profile of the state-sponsored efforts to move from timber to tourism: **Grays Harbor Historical Seaport** (daily; $3; 360/532-8611), a mile south of Hwy-12. A reconstruction of one of American explorer Capt. Robert Gray's ships, the *Lady Washington,* can be toured—when she's

The *Lady Washington* is a replica of one of the first American ships to explore the West Coast.

not off on one of her regular "goodwill" cruises. The original ship was the first American vessel to visit the area, way back in 1788, and the replica was completed here in 1989 to celebrate the Washington State centennial.

Grunge-rock hero and Nirvana lead singer Kurt Cobain grew up in and around Aberdeen, as did ace road-trip photographer Lee Friedlander.

The region's long-time employer, the Weyerhaeuser pulp mill, located alongside US-101 in the inappropriately named town of Cosmopolis, closed down in 2009. Heading south from Aberdeen, a coastal loop runs along the Pacific via Hwy-105, while US-101 cuts inland, south toward Raymond and Willapa Bay. Heading east from Aberdeen, US-12 cuts inland, passing the defunct Satsop nuclear power plant and one of the most heavily logged areas in Washington before joining the I-5 freeway south of the state capital of Olympia. Midway along, the **Grays Harbor Hostel** in Elma (360/482-3119) has $18-a-night beds (and a small Frisbee golf course!).

Hwy-105: Westport and Tokeland

Between Hoquiam and Raymond, US-101 cuts inland from the coast, while an alternative route, Hwy-105, loops to the west past miles of cranberry bogs (and occasional wild elk) through the salmon-fishing town of **Westport.** Once called "The Salmon Capital of the World," and still a prime place for watching migrating gray whales, Westport is a very busy port—and

one of Washington's few good surfing, clam-digging, and surf-kayaking beaches. The whole place really comes to life during the Labor Day seafood festival, but any time of the year the best stop is **Brady's Oysters** (360/268-0077), at the foot of the Hwy-105 bridge from Aberdeen.

At the south edge of the peninsula, absorb more coastal character at the 1885 **Tokeland Hotel** ($43–65; 360/267-7006), off Hwy-105 on the north shore of Willapa Bay, with old-fashioned lodgings (shared bathrooms) and a cozy old dining room.

Willapa Bay: Raymond and South Bend

One of the country's prime oystering grounds, **Willapa Bay** is sheltered from the Pacific by the Long Beach Peninsula and fed by the Nasalle, Willapa, and North Fall Rivers. There are very few towns or even villages on this stretch of US-101, which winds past tidal marshes, cattle ranches, and extensively clear-cut forests—which billboards proclaim to be "America's first industrial tree farm," giving dates of harvest, planting, and re-harvest, on a roughly 40-year cycle.

If the weather's right for a picnic, fresh shellfish can be had at bargain prices—live in the shell, or pre-shucked by the half gallon—from the area's many producers, wholesalers, and roadside stands. Look for them all along US-101 and up the Long Beach peninsula.

At the northeast corner of Willapa Bay, on the south bank of the Willapa River, stand two towns that jointly embody the natural resource–based history and economy of the Pacific Northwest: **Raymond** (pop. 2,882) has the lumber mills, while **South Bend** (pop. 1,637) calls itself the "Oyster Capital of the World." South Bend's other claim to fame is its landmark **Pacific County Courthouse** (Mon.–Fri. only), which since 1910 has loomed like a mini Taj Mahal on a hill just east of US-101. Step inside for a look at the 30-foot stained-glass dome above the rotunda, and wander through the lushly landscaped park next door.

If you want to stretch your legs, Raymond and South Bend are linked by the very nice Chehalis Trail, a walking and cycling path that follows an old railroad right-of-way along the Willapa River, amidst some engaging roadside metal sculptures of people canoeing, bird-watching, cycling, fishing, and generally enjoying the great outdoors.

Long Beach Peninsula

On the western side of Willapa Bay, the **Long Beach Peninsula** stretches for 28 miles of hard-packed sandy beaches along the

"World's Largest Frying Pan"

roiling Pacific Ocean. Away from the few small towns, beaches and breakers abound along here, and you won't have any problem finding peace and solitude. The center of activity on the Long Beach Peninsula is the town of **Long Beach,** two miles from US-101, with a wanderable collection of crafts galleries and souvenir shops. A short walk west from "downtown" Long Beach, a wooden boardwalk winds along the coastal dunes, leading to a very rare sight: the reconstructed skeleton of a gray whale. Lewis and Clark saw similar bones when they passed by 200-plus years ago, and a Discovery Trail linking Corps of Discovery locations runs from here south to Ilwaco, near the mouth of the Columbia River.

If you can bear to stretch your budget a little, Long Beach is home to one of the coast's best B&Bs, historic **The Shelburne Inn** ($115 and up; 4415 Pacific Way; 360/642-2442), located in the Seaview neighborhood (Pacific Way is also known as Hwy-103, the main road). The Shelburne Inn also houses a friendly pub. Long Beach is also the home of the nearly-10-feet-in-diameter "World's Largest Frying Pan," which sits on a rack across from the one-of-a-kind **Marsh's Free Museum** (409 S. Pacific Ave.; 360/642-2188), a totally tacky (and wonderfully kitsch) collection of postcards, peep shows, and old-time arcade games.

The rest of the slender Long Beach peninsula is quite quiet, dotted with cranberry bogs and historic fishing and oystering towns. In **Nahcotta,** a dozen miles north of Long Beach, you can stay overnight at the cozy **Moby Dick Hotel and Oyster Farm** ($90–150; 25814 Sandridge Rd.; 360/665-4543), where they grow, harvest, and serve their own bivalve treats. Just north, **Oysterville** is the peninsula's oldest community, with some nifty historic homes dating back to the 1850s. The peninsula comes to an end in the north at **Leadbetter Point State Park,** a great place for watching gulls, hawks, eagles, and migratory seabirds passing through on the Pacific Flyway.

Cape Disappointment

The high headland marking the place where the Columbia River finally merges into the Pacific Ocean, **Cape Disappointment** was named by the early explorer Capt. John Meares, who in 1788 incorrectly interpreted the treacherous sandbars offshore to mean that, despite reports to the contrary, there was neither a major river nor any mythical Northwest Passage here.

Besides the grand view of the raging ocean, the best reason to visit the cape is to tour the small but worthwhile **Lewis and Clark Interpretive Center** (daily; $5; 360/642-3029), incongruously built atop a World War II–era artillery emplacement a short walk from the end of the road. On November 7, 1805, after five months and more than 4,000 miles, the explorers finally laid eyes on the Pacific from this point, and then they sat through nine days of continuous rain before fleeing south to Oregon. Displays inside the museum give the overall context for their journey of discovery, walking you through the different stages of their two-year round-trip. The small "Cape D" lighthouse stands atop a cliff, a half-mile walk from the Lewis and Clark museum, which is 200 feet above the Pacific Ocean. The more impressively photogenic North Head Lighthouse, on the ocean side of the peninsula a mile north of the museum, is the oldest on the West Coast.

Two statues sculpted by chain saws, in a small state park three miles west of the US-101 bridge across the Columbia River, mark the site where Lewis and Clark camped in December 1805 before heading south in search of better weather—which is about the only thing they never found on their epic trip.

The entire 1,882-acre area around the cape, including miles of beaches backed by rugged cliffs, is protected from development within **Cape Disappointment State Park** (360/642-3029), which has hiking, camping, and overnight lodgings in historic quarters next to North Head Lighthouse.

In recent years there have been a number of developments building on the area's Lewis and Clark connections, including the eight-mile Discovery Trail, which heads north to the town of Long Beach, and a series of thought-provoking installations by architect Maya Lin (creator of the Washington, D.C., Vietnam Veterans Memorial). Called the Confluence Project, and located mostly along the riverfront east of the museum, these works all deal with the coming together of the natural and man-made worlds, as well as the interaction of explorers and Native Americans. The installations range from boardwalks and interpretive trails (lined in places by quotations from Lewis and Clark's diaries) to a sculptural basalt "fish-cleaning" table.

The nearest services to Cape Disappointment—gas stations and a couple of cafés—are two miles away, back on US-101 in the rough-and-tumble fishing port of **Ilwaco,** where you can also enjoy the sophisticated yet simple and fresh seafood prepared at **Pelicano Restaurant** (177 Howerton Way SE; 360/642-4034), on the harbor.

Southeast of Ilwaco, toward the Oregon border, US-101 winds along the north bank of the Columbia River, giving good views of the mighty river's five-mile-wide mouth.

OREGON

Rarely losing sight of the Pacific Ocean during its 340-mile jaunt along the Oregon coast, US-101 winds past rock-bound coast, ancient forests, and innumerable towns and villages. While the region also has its share of strip towns and places where the timber boom went bust, the beach loops, historic restorations, and more state parks per mile than any place in the country soften its few hard edges. Every 20 miles or so, you'll pass through attractive, if moderately touristy, towns populated by at most a few thousand people, but as a general rule it's the mileage between these hamlets that explains why most people visit: to take in one of the most dramatic meetings of rock and tide in the world.

Starting in the north along the Columbia River at historic **Astoria,** one of the oldest settlements in the western United States, the route winds along the ocean past the very different beachfront hamlets of **Seaside** and **Cannon Beach** before edging slightly inland through the rich dairy lands of **Tillamook County.** Midway along, the popular vacation spots of **Lincoln City, Newport,** and **Florence** form the most developed corridor along the coast, but it's still easy to reach unpeopled stretches, especially at the remarkable **Oregon Dunes** stretching to the south. The dunes end abruptly at the heavily industrial port of **Coos Bay,** beyond which

Much as Forks, Washington, has benefited from its connections with the *Twilight* books and films, Astoria gets a boost in tourism numbers thanks to its starring role in the 1980s Steven Spielberg teen adventure film *The Goonies.*

the natural beauty returns with a string of state parks and the diverse coastal towns of **Bandon, Port Orford, Gold Beach,** and **Brookings.**

Astoria

The oldest American city west of the Rockies, **Astoria** (pop. 9,477) is an upbeat mix of lovingly preserved past and busy contemporary commerce. Houses perched atop high hills overlook the Columbia River, creating a favorite backdrop for Hollywood movies. Despite its picturesque appearance, Astoria supports an active commercial fishing fleet, and dozens of tugboats guide tankers and container ships across the treacherous sandbars. Founded by and named after fur-trade magnate John Jacob Astor in 1811, Astoria protected the tenuous American claim to the Pacific coast until the opening of the Oregon Trail brought substantial settlement. By the turn of the 20th century, Astoria was still Oregon's second-largest city, but the downturn in both salmon fishing and logging since the end of World War II has caused an economic decline that, as always, town officials look to tourism to overcome.

US-101 crosses the Columbia River on the toll-free, high-level Astoria-Megler Bridge, completed in 1966, which drops you at the west end of the downtown waterfront. To get a sense of the lay of the land, follow the signs along 16th Street up Coxcomb Hill to the **Astoria Column** (daily dawn–dusk; $1 per car) for a view of the Columbia meeting the ocean, the coastal plain south to Tillamook Head, and the snowcapped Cascade Range (including, on a clear day, Mt. St. Helens) on the eastern horizon. A mosaic chronicling local history is wrapped like a ribbon around the column, tracing

To find out about local issues and current events on the northern Oregon coast, pick up a copy of the excellent **Daily Astorian** newspaper, or tune to commercial-free **KMUN 91.5 FM** for NPR news and diverse programming.

the many significant events in the town's past. A spiral staircase climbs to the top.

Back downtown **Flavel House Museum** (daily; $5; 441 8th St.) is a Queen Anne–style Victorian showplace restored as an elegantly furnished museum of Astoria's first millionaire, Columbia River pilot George Flavel. A half mile east, near the foot of 17th Street on the north side of waterfront Marine Drive, the **Columbia River Maritime Museum** (daily; $10; 503/325-2323) displays a large and very impressive collection that tells the story of the lifeblood of this community: the Columbia River.

Fortify yourself at one of the many good seafood places along the water, starting at the funky, ever-popular **Columbian Café** (1114 Marine Dr.; 503/325-2233), where chef Uriah Hulsey prepares all sorts of ultra-fresh food in an impossibly cramped galley kitchen. Meals are massive yet reasonably priced, so be sure to arrive with an appetite; breakfast and lunch are served Wednesday–Sunday, dinner Wednesday–Saturday. Another Astoria eating option is the casual **Ship Inn** (503/325-0033), serving halibut fish-and-chips under the bridge at Marine Drive and 2nd Street. Foodies might want to visit adjacent **Josephson's Smokehouse** (106 Marine Dr.; 503/325-2190) to sample the delicious array of smoked salmon, which is prepared on the premises and sold all over the country.

To absorb a full portion of Astoria's addictive ambience, stay the night at the riverview **Crest Motel** ($65 and up; 5366 Leif Erickson Dr.; 503/325-3141), three miles east of town along US-30, or in town at the luxurious and historic **Hotel Elliott** ($129 and up; 357 12th St.; 877/378-1924). Astoria also has a handful of nice B&Bs like the 1890s **Astoria Inn Bed and Breakfast** ($80 and up; 3391 Irving Ave.; 503/325-8153).

Fort Clatsop

In the conifer forests six miles south of Astoria and three miles east of US-101, and part of the extensive Lewis and Clark National Historical Park, the **Fort Clatsop National Memorial** (daily; $3 per person; 503/861-2471) is a credible reconstruction of the encampment Lewis and Clark and company constructed during the winter of 1805–1806. Now the centerpiece of the sprawling, multi-state Lewis and Clark National Historical Park, Fort Clatsop

Fort Stevens, off US-101 on the way to Fort Clatsop, was the only continental U.S. fortification bombed during World War II, sustaining a shelling from a Japanese submarine on June 21, 1942.

has been fully (and in many ways more accurately) rebuilt after a 2005 fire destroyed the first (circa 1955) replica. The fort itself is joined by a range of exhibits in the visitors center. A longer (13-mile round-trip) trail leads to the coast, and summertime costumed rangers help conjure the travails of two centuries ago. The expedition spent three miserable months here, mingling occasionally with the native Clatsop and Chinook tribes but mostly growing moldy in the incessant rain and damp while being bitten by fleas, sewing new moccasins, and making salt in preparation for the return journey across the continent.

Gearhart

In between burly Astoria and the boisterous beach resort of Seaside, but a world away from its neighbors in terms of character and ambience, the tiny town of **Gearhart** (pop. 1,462) was the summer vacation home of influential chef and cookbook author James Beard. Beard's culinary legacy lives on in the **Pacific Way Bakery & Cafe** (601 Pacific Way; 503/738-0245), a half mile west of US-101, which offers the coast's best coffees and croissants, along with four-star lunches and dinners. Like many places along the Oregon coast, it's closed Tuesday and Wednesday.

Seaside

Nothing along the Oregon coast prepares you for the carnival ambience of downtown **Seaside** (pop. 6,457), one of Oregon's oldest seafront resorts. Ben Holladay, who built a resort here in the 1870s, included a racetrack, zoo, and plush hotel to lure Portlanders to ride his rail line to the beach. Come during spring break, or on a weekend during July or August, and join the 50,000 or more visitors wandering among the saltwater-taffy stands and video-game arcades along Broadway, or cruising the concrete boardwalk (called The Prom) along the beach.

statue of explorers Lewis and Clark at the end of the trail in Seaside

centennial commemorative stamp

Portland

Portland, Oregon's largest city, is located inland from the coast near the confluence of the Willamette and Columbia Rivers. Due to its strategic location, the pioneer municipality grew so fast it was nicknamed Stumptown for the hundreds of fir stumps left by early loggers, and while railroad tracks and other heavy industrial remnants are still highly visible around town, Portland's riverfront park and numerous winding greenways show that this mini metropolis is not a smokestack town but a community that values art and nature as highly as commerce. Along with the largest (5,000-acre Forest Park) and the smallest (24-inches-in-diameter Mill Ends Park) urban parks in the nation, and one of the coolest urban skate parks anywhere (under the Burnside Bridge), Portland also has more movie theaters, restaurants, microbreweries, and bookstores per capita than any other U.S. city.

The oldest part of Portland has, over the past few years, been renovated into a lively Old Town district, where cast-iron facades of 120-year-old buildings hold some of the city's most popular bars, clubs, and cafés. (Not to mention general weirdness magnets like the 24-Hour Church of Elvis, most recently found at 408 N.W. Couch Street.) South of Old Town along the river, an ugly freeway has been torn down to form the mile-long Tom McCall Waterfront Park, and west of the river, downtown Portland centers on lively Pioneer Courthouse Square, at 6th Avenue and Yamhill Street. South of the square, the South Park Blocks between Park and Ninth Avenues were set aside as parklands in the original city plan and are now bounded by Portland's prime museums. One essential Portland place is north of the square: **Powell's Books** (503/228-0540), at 1005 W. Burnside Street across from the Blitz-Weinhard Brewery, is the largest (and certainly among the best) new-and-used bookshop in the world.

One of the largest and oldest ballparks in the minor leagues, the circa-1926 Civic Stadium, downtown off Burnside at 1844 SW Morrison, has been fully renovated and redubbed PGE Park, home to the **Portland Beavers** (503/553-5555), the San Diego Padres' top farm club.

Along the river south of town, **Oaks Park** (503/233-5777) is a wonderful circa-1905 amusement park, with ancient and modern thrill rides all packed together in a sylvan, oak tree–dotted park.

Practicalities

Air travelers can land at Portland International Airport (PDX), but most long-distance flights here come and go via Seattle's Sea-Tac, which is only about 2.5 hours' drive north, via the I-5 freeway. Getting around public-spirited Portland is a breeze thanks to the combination of an efficient bus system and a light rail train (called MAX; 503/238-7433).

Though it doesn't have a trendy reputation, Portland does have some great restaurants in all stripes and sizes. **Esparza's Tex-Mex,** 2725 SE Ankeny Street (503/234-7909), hidden away behind a hole-in-the-wall facade a block south of E. Burnside Street, is worth searching out for its smoky pork tacos and a jukebox featuring Tejano, norteño, and Marty Robbins hits. For more traditional Portland fare, head to **Jake's Famous Crawfish** (503/226-1419), at 401 SW 12th Street, which for over a century has been the place to go for the finest, freshest seafood. For meat, nothing beats the **Ringside** (503/223-1513), near PGE Park at 2165 W. Burnside Street, long famous for its great beef, fine fried chicken, monster Walla Walla sweet onion rings, and Hemingway-esque ambience. If your taste happens to run more to Marilyn Manson than Marilyn Monroe, you'll probably prefer to eat across town at **Dots Cafe** (503/235-0203), at 2521 SE Clinton Street, a late-night hangout that has comfy dark booths, great black-bean burritos, microbrews, and pool tables.

There are all sorts of places to stay in Portland, starting with a pair of popular **HI-Portland Hostels,** one east of downtown at 3031 Hawthorne Boulevard (503/236-3380) and a newer one in the Northwest District, at 425 NW 18th Avenue (503/241-2783). The stylish, comfortable, and close-to-downtown **Hotel DeLuxe** ($150 and up; 503/219-2094) is a newly renovated boutique hotel at 729 SW 15th Avenue. If you feel like splurging, try another impeccably restored downtown landmark, the **Heathman Hotel** ($199 and up; 503/241-4100 or 800/551-0011), at 1009 SW Broadway, with an elegant lobby and sumptuously appointed (if somewhat small) rooms.

The best source of visitor information on Portland is the **Portland Visitors Association** (503/275-9750 or 800/962-3700), on Pioneer Courthouse Square.

Where Broadway meets the beach, a small traffic circle known locally as The Turnaround is marked by a statue and a sign proclaiming the town "The End of the Lewis and Clark Trail." South of here, between Beach Drive and The Prom, is a replica of the Lewis and Clark salt cairn, where the explorers boiled seawater nonstop for seven weeks to produce enough salt to preserve meat for their return trip east. From the south end of Seaside, you can follow a challenging but very rewarding five-mile trail over Tillamook Head to Ecola State Park.

A half mile north of downtown, housed in a wood-shingled old motor court on the banks of the Necanicum River, the **Seaside International Hostel** (930 N. Holladay Dr.; 503/738-7911) has dorm beds, private rooms, canoes and kayaks, an espresso bar, and nightly movies. There are dozens of motels and a handful of B&Bs in Seaside, booked solid in summer and serene, verging on lonely, come wintertime.

Ecola State Park

Just north of Cannon Beach, a mile south of the junction between US-101 and US-26 from Portland, the rainforested access road through **Ecola State Park** (day use only; $5 per car; 503/436-2844) leads you to one of the most photographed views on the coast: Looking south you can see Haystack Rock and Cannon Beach with Neahkahnie Mountain looming above them. Out to sea, the sight of **Tillamook Rock Lighthouse** to the northwest is also striking. Operational from 1881 to 1957, the lighthouse is now used as a repository for the ashes of people who've been cremated.

The rest of Ecola State Park protects a series of rugged headlands stretching for nine miles along the coast, with many forested hiking trails, including some of the most scenic portions of the Oregon Coast Trail system. The park also marks the southernmost extent of Lewis and Clark's cross-country expedition. Clark and a few other members of the Corps of Discovery expedition traversed the area in search of supplements to their diet of hardtack and dried salmon. The word *"ecola"* means whale in the Chinookan tongue and was affixed to this region by the Lewis and Clark expedition, who found one of these leviathans washed up on a beach. They happily bought 300 pounds of tangy whale blubber from local Indians, but these days you'd better bring your own lunch to picnic atop bluffs with sweeping views of the rock-strewn Pacific. The view from the top of **Tillamook Head,** which rises 1,200 feet above the sea at the heart of the park, was memorialized by explorer William Clark as "the grandest and most pleasing prospect" he had ever beheld.

Cannon Beach

Unlike many Oregon coast towns, **Cannon Beach** (pop. 1,690) is hidden from the highway, but it's one place you won't want to miss. Though it's little more than a stone's throw south of boisterous Seaside, Cannon Beach has long been known as an artists' colony, and while it has grown considerably in recent years thanks to its popularity as a weekend escape from Portland, it retains a peaceful, rustic atmosphere.

Every summer, Cannon Beach hosts one of the largest and most enjoyable **sand castle competitions** on the West Coast, with some 10,000 spectators and as many as 1,000 participants turning out with their buckets and spades. In terms of traditional tourist attractions, there's not a lot to do, but Cannon Beach is an unbeatable place in which to stop and unwind, or to take long walks along the nine-mile strand and then retreat indoors to the many good galleries, cafés, and restaurants. For breakfast or brunch, fill up on eggs Benedict at **The Lazy Susan Cafe** (closed Tues.; 126 N. Hemlock Street; 503/436-2816); it also serves a stupendous array of ice cream at its "scoop shop" up the street. Another great, casual gourmet place to eat is **Ecola Seafoods** (208 N. Spruce St.; 503/436-9130), which serves locally caught fish and shellfish—including an excellent $5 chowder.

Cannon Beach

Reasonably priced rooms near the beach and town can be found at the oceanfront **Sea Sprite at Haystack Rock** ($99 and up; 280 S. Nebesna St.; 503/436-2266).

South of Cannon Beach, the beach loop runs along a spectacular grouping of volcanic basalt plugs, notably 235-foot-high **Haystack Rock.** Elsewhere along the Oregon coast, there are at least two more geological outcrops called Haystack Rock, a bigger one off Cape Kiwanda and another down near Bandon.

Neahkahnie Mountain and Oswald West State Park

South of Cannon Beach, US-101 rises high above the Pacific. Nowhere else along the Oregon coast does the roadbed offer such a sweeping ocean view. Soaring another thousand feet above the highway is **Neahkahnie Mountain,** which offers unsurpassed views up and down the coast. About 10 miles south of Cannon Beach at **Oswald West State Park** (800/551-6949), a half-mile trail winds beneath the highway through an ancient forest to driftwood-laden (and surfer-friendly) Short Sands Beach and the tidepools of Smuggler's Cove. Named for an early governor of Oregon who successfully proposed preserving and protecting the beaches of Oregon as state (rather than private) property, Oswald West State Park is a good start for longer hikes, to weather-beaten Cape Falcon or across US-101 to the summit of Neahkahnie Mountain.

South of Neahkahnie Mountain, and thus spared much of the stormy coastal weather (annual rainfall hereabouts averages more than 80 inches), is the upscale resort town of **Manzanita.** Nearby **Nehalem Bay State Park** (503/368-5154) has a large campground with hundreds of sites and plenty of hot showers. US-101 continues through a series of small towns before winding inland past the sloughs and dairy country along Tillamook Bay.

Tillamook

Tillamook (pop. 4,400), where cows outnumber people, sprawls over lush grasslands at the southern end of Tillamook Bay. Its motto, "Land of cheese, trees, and ocean breeze," conjures a clear sense of a place where the high school

Tillamook Cheese Factory

football team is cheered on by shouts of "Go Cheesemakers!" Tillamook (a Salish word meaning "land of many waters") is dominated by the **Tillamook Cheese Factory** at the north end of town, one of the busiest tourist draws in the state. Inside, a self-guided tour with informational placards traces Tillamook cheese-making from the last century to the present, and a glassed-in observation area lets you watch the stuff being made and packaged.

Tillamook's other attraction is east of US-101 and south of town. One of the world's largest wooden structures—296 feet wide, 1,072 feet long, and nearly 200 feet tall, enclosing more than seven acres of open-span floor space—has been preserved as the **Tillamook Air Museum** (daily; $9 adults; 503/842-1130). Built in 1942, the structure is now a museum telling the story of the World War II surveillance blimps kept here by the U.S. Navy. There are also displays about other dirigible craft (like the ill-fated *Hindenburg*) as well as a world-class collection of vintage airplanes (from MiG fighters to an elegant, twin-tailed P-38 Lightning), plus a theater and a restaurant, all making for a fascinating and unusual stop. The building used to be one of a pair of hangars, but the other one burned down in 1992.

Three Capes Loop

US-101 veers inland for 50 miles between Tillamook and Lincoln City, the next sizable town south. If time and weather are on your side, head west along the coast via the well-signed, 40-mile-long **Three Capes Loop.** Running northwest from Tillamook, the loop reaches the mouth of Tillamook Bay at **Cape Meares,** which has a restored 1890 lighthouse and an oddly contorted Sitka spruce known as the Octopus Tree.

Heading south through the coastal villages of **Oceanside** and **Netarts,** the loop proceeds through dairy country until it climbs onto the shoulder of **Cape Lookout,** where a small sign proclaiming Wildlife Viewing Area marks the beginning of a 2.5-mile trail that leads through an ancient forest to the tip of the cape, 100-plus feet above the water. Besides the coastal panorama, in winter and spring this is a prime place to view passing gray whales. From the trailhead, the middle path leads to the

Seven miles south of Tillamook, a turnoff east follows a bumpy, one-mile access road leading to the highest waterfall in Oregon's Coast Range, 319-foot **Munson Creek Falls.** From the parking area at the end of the road, a short trail leads to this year-round cascade.

cape, while others to the left and right lead down to the water. **Cape Lookout State Park** (503/842-4981) has the area's most popular campground, where tent sites, yurts, and cabins come with hot showers and other creature comforts.

The Oregon coast's most famous promontory, **Cape Kiwanda,** sees some of the state's wildest surf battering the sandstone headland. Across from the cape is yet another **Haystack Rock,** this one being a 327-foot-tall sea stack, a half mile offshore. Along the beach south of the cape, surfers ride waves while fisherfolk skid their small dories along the sands most afternoons—a sight worth hanging around to see.

The southernmost settlement on this scenic alternative to US-101 is neighboring **Pacific City,** where two great places to eat, **The Grateful Bread Bakery** (503/965-7337) and the **Riverhouse** (503/965-6722), sit beachside on Brooten Road.

Lincoln City

The most developed section of the Oregon coast stretches for miles along US-101 through **Lincoln City** (pop. 7,930), seven miles of strip malls, outlet stores, fast-food franchises, and motels. With more than 1,000 oceanside rooms, Lincoln City does offer some of the coast's cheapest lodging, especially in the off-season when sign after sign advertises rooms for as low as $35 a night. Along with inexpensive accommodations, Lincoln City has some great places to eat. Start the day with a huge breakfast at **The Beach Dog Café** (1266 SW 50th St.; 541/996-3647), and after a day on the beach or in the forests, tuck into some four-star fish tacos, chowders, or battered seafood at **J's Fish 'N' Chips** (1800 SE US-101; 541/994-4445).

South of Lincoln City, 2.5 miles east of US-101, the **Drift Creek Covered Bridge** is the oldest of some 50 such structures in the state.

One more unforgettable culinary attraction hereabouts sits five miles northeast of Lincoln City, just east of US-101 on Hwy-18, the main road to and from Portland: the **Otis Café** (1259 Salmon River Hwy.; 541/994-2813), which immortalizes American road food, offering excellent waffles and other breakfast treats along with epicurean lunches and fresh berry pies for dessert. The Otis Café is open for breakfast, lunch, and dinner daily.

Seven miles south of Lincoln City, a sign announces the **Salishan Spa & Golf Resort** (800/452-2300), a beautifully landscaped rustic golf resort with a five-star dining room and a surprisingly affordable more-casual restaurant, **The Sun Room.**

Down the hill across US-101, **Siletz Bay** is a bird-watcher's paradise, where hawks and herons and thousands of other seabirds (along with chinook salmon and cutthroat trout) are protected within a federal wildlife refuge.

Depoe Bay

Depoe Bay has an appeal, but so much of its natural beauty is obscured from the highway by gift shops or intruded upon by traffic that you've got to know where to look. In his book *Blue Highways,* William Least Heat-Moon wrote "Depoe Bay used to be a pictur-

Depoe Bay was originally known as Depot Bay, named after a local Siletz Indian who worked at the local U.S. Army depot and called himself Charlie Depot.

esque fishing village; now it was just picturesque." While it's true that most of the commercial fishing is long gone, you can still park your car along the highway and walk out on the bridge to watch sportfishing boats move through the narrow channel to what the *Guinness Book of Records* rates as the world's smallest navigable natural harbor. South of the bridge is another record-setter, the Oregon coast's largest secondhand bookstore, the **Channel Bookstore** (541/765-2352).

The **Sea Hag** restaurant (541/765-2734), on US-101 in downtown Depoe Bay, is a time-tested breakfast place, and people drive for miles to enjoy the pies at the **Spouting Horn** (541/765-2261), overlooking the harbor. For a place to stay, try the very popular **Inn at Arch Rock** ($69 and up; 70 NW Sunset St.; 800/767-1835).

Cape Foulweather and the Devil's Punchbowl

Between Depoe Bay and Newport, the roadside scenery along US-101 and the parallel "old road," now signed as the Otter Crest Loop, is dominated by miles of broad beaches and sandstone bluffs, including the 500-foot headland of **Cape Foulweather,** named by Capt. James Cook and offering a 360-degree coastal panorama. The Otter Crest Loop has frequently been closed by slides and reconstruction efforts, but you can reach it from many access roads. With fine old bridges and numerous vistas, it's a great drive—or bicycle route.

Farther south, mid way between Depoe Bay and Newport, the aptly named **Devil's Punchbowl** gives a ringside seat on a frothy confrontation between rock and tide. In the parking area you'll find a small lunch café (a branch of Newport's **Mo's**), whose claim to fame remains a visit from Bruce Springsteen on June 11, 1987.

inside the aquarium tunnel at the Oregon Coast Aquarium

Newport

Another old fishing community turned tourist nexus, **Newport** (pop. 9,989) became popular in the 1860s on the strength of sweet-tasting Yaquina Bay oysters, which were in demand from San Francisco to New York City and are still available at local restaurants. Oysters, crabs, and clams, along with sea otters, sea lions, sharks, and seabirds, are the stars of the show at the large and modern **Oregon Coast Aquarium** (daily; $16; 541/867-3474), south of Newport across the Yaquina Bay Bridge. The aquarium includes an aquatic aviary, where tufted puffins and other shore-birds cavort in a simulated rockbound coastal habitat, and over 40,000 square feet of similarly eco-friendly exhibits, many of them outdoors.

The coast and inland forests along the Siletz River near Depoe Bay and Newport were the primary location of the Ken Kesey novels and films *One Flew Over the Cuckoo's Nest* and *Sometimes a Great Notion.*

The old-growth forests of the **Drift Creek Wilderness** east of Waldport are prime nesting areas for the endangered northern spotted owl, whose numbers are still declining.

On the north side of the US-101 bridge over Yaquina Bay, turn onto Hurbert Street and head for the bayfront, where boatyards and fish-packing plants service a working harbor. Though it's still one of the state's largest fishing ports, much of Newport's bayfront has been con-sumed by souvenir shops, a wax mu-seum, a Ripley's Believe It or Not,

and other tourist traps. But you'll find the original **Mo's** (622 SW Bay Blvd.; 541/265-2979), a locally famous seafood restaurant.

North of the harbor is **Nye Beach,** an interesting mélange of old-fashioned beach houses and destination resorts on the western side of US-101. Nye Beach is home to hotels, motels, and the bohemian **Sylvia Beach Hotel** ($70–up; 267 NW Cliff St.; 541/265-5428), *the* place to stay in Newport for anyone of literary bent. If you can't afford the private rooms—with decor evocative of different authors—there are dormitory bunk beds for around $40 a night. All rates include breakfast, and sumptuous dinners are available, too.

Waldport

If you want to avoid lines and general tourist bustle, **Waldport** is a nice alternative to the resort towns surrounding it. Tourism is low-key here, and you can still sense the vestiges of the resource-based economy, a by-product of the town's proximity to rich timber stands and superlative fishing. Stop along US-101 at the **Alsea Bay Historic Interpretive Center** (541/563-2002) for interesting exhibits on coastal transportation and the local Alsea tribe, as well as a telescope trained on waterfowl and seals in the bay. The center sits at the southwest foot of the modern span that, in 1991, replaced the historic (circa-1936) art deco–style bridge. From the north end of the bridge, you can follow Hwy-34 seven miles upstream to **JD's Café at Kozy Kove** (541/528-3725), a floating restaurant with good food and a bucolic riverside ambience.

A little more than two miles south of Waldport, **Cape Cod Cottages** ($65–185; 4150 SW Pacific Coast Hwy.; 541/563-2106) is a good choice for location and comfort. Four miles south of Waldport, halfway to Yachats, **Beachside State Park** (541/563-3220) has a very popular campground, with hot showers, RV hookups, and a lovely stretch of sandy beach.

Yachats

On the way into **Yachats** (pop. 690; pronounced "YA-hots"), beach loops on either side of the Yachats River give a sense of why the area is called "the gem of the Oregon coast." It's a great place to wander and get lost and found again, especially at the beautiful Ocean Road State Natural Site, where incredible views along a one-mile loop road look out over crashing waves, tide-pools, blowholes, and, in winter, gray whales migrating offshore.

Back in town, for the past 30-plus years, **Leroy's Blue Whale** (580 Hwy-101 N., 541/547-3399), on US-101, has been serving breakfast, lunch, and dinner every day, featuring fluffy pancakes, fresh chowders, and fine fish-and-chips.

The word "cottage" is a popular lodging label around Yachats, usually referring to a moderately priced, self-contained cabin or duplex with kitchen. On US-101 there are a half dozen different cottage complexes, each fronting the beach. If you want more than a simple place to spend the night, the **Oregon House** ($65 and up; 541/547-3329) on US-101 nine miles south of Yachats has spacious apartment-like rooms, some with fireplaces and ocean views, and all with access to the well-tended grounds and trails leading down the bluffs to a gem of a sandy cove.

Cape Perpetua

For more than 300 miles along the Oregon coast, US-101 abounds with national forests, state parks, and viewpoints. But unless you have your whole lifetime to spend here, **Cape Perpetua,** two miles south of Yachats, deserves most of your attention. Stop first at the **Cape Perpetua Visitor Center** (541/547-3289), just east of US-101, for seacoast views and exhibits on forestry and area history. From the visitors center, trails lead across the highway past wind-bent trees, piles of seashells and other artifacts left behind by native peoples, excellent tide-pools, and two rock formations: Spouting Horn and the Devil's Churn. During stormy seas, both shoot huge spouts of foam into the air. The friendly folks at the visitors center can also point you toward Cape Perpetua's very attractive campground.

You can reach the top of 800-foot-high Cape Perpetua itself by following a two-mile-long road, marked by Cape Perpetua Viewpoint signs and leaving US-101 100 yards or so north of the visitors center. Once atop the cape, walk the **Whispering Spruce Trail,** a half-mile loop around the rim of the promontory that yields, on a clear day, 150-mile views of the Oregon coast from a rustic, WPA-built stone observation point.

Heceta Head and the Sea Lion Caves

Halfway between Cape Perpetua and Florence, a small bridge just south of Carl G. Washburne Memorial State Park marks the turnoff to **Heceta Head** lighthouse, perhaps the most photographed beacon in the United States. Built in 1894, it was named for the Spanish mariner who is credited with being the first European to set foot in the region. You'll have to be content with gazing at it across the cove from a small but rarely crowded beach, unless you stay at the quaint old lighthouse keeper's quarters, restored as an unforgettable B&B ($133 and up; 541/547-3696).

A half-mile south of Heceta Head lighthouse, 11 miles north of Florence, traffic along US-101 slows to a stop at the gift shop that serves as the entrance to **Sea Lion Caves** (daily; $12). You can ride an elevator down to the world's largest sea cave, the only mainland rookery for the Steller sea lion. Fall and winter offer the best times to see (and smell!) these animals, which throng together here during mating season. When the weather's nice, you can often watch them swimming in the ocean (for free, without the seal smells . . .) from a viewpoint 100 yards up US-101.

Florence

If first and last impressions are enduring, **Florence** is truly blessed. As you enter the city from the north, US-101 climbs high above the ocean; coming from the south, travelers are greeted by the graceful **Siuslaw River Bridge,** perhaps the most impressive of a handful of WPA-built spans designed by Conde McCullough and decorated with his trademark Egyptian obelisks and art deco stylings. Unfortunately, first impressions feel a little misleading, since much of

LOOKING TOWARD TEN MILE LAKE AND SUTTON LAKE

what you can see from US-101 is a bland highway sprawl of motels, gas stations, and franchised restaurants.

The best part of Florence, **Old Town,** is just upstream from that landmark bridge, along the north bank of the Siuslaw River. Here, among Bay Street's three blocks of interesting boutiques and galleries, you'll find a number of cafés and seafood restaurants. Old Town Florence is also home to the very welcoming **Edwin K B&B** ($125–200; 1155 Bay St.; 541/997-8360), a lovely white Craftsman-style home built in 1914 by one of the town's founders.

Back along US-101, car culture fans will relish the chance to eat burgers and fries at **Bliss' Hot Rod Grill,** a mile north of Old Town (1179 US-101; 541/997-6726), where walls are covered in old road signs and some of the spacious booths are made from classic 1950s American cars.

"Dune Country": Oregon's Sahara

For nearly 50 miles south of Florence, US-101 has an extensive panorama of oceanfront dunes. Though the dunes are often obscured from view by forests, roadside signs indicate access roads to numerous dunescapes on both sides of the highway. Coming from the north, the first of these access points is **Jessie M. Honeyman Memorial State Park,** three miles south of

Florence, where rhododendrons line a trail leading to a 150-foot-high dune overlooking a mirage-like lake.

Before setting out on any extended exploration, your first stop should be the USFS-run **Oregon Dunes National Recreation Area Visitors Center** (541/271-3611) at the junction of US-101 and Hwy-38 in **Reedsport,** along the Umpqua River midway between Florence and Coos Bay at the heart of the dunes. The helpful rangers can provide detailed information on hiking and camping throughout the park. Reedsport itself has a line of motels and burger joints—**Don's Main Street Family Restaurant** (2115 Winchester Ave.; 541/271-2032), on US-101, has legions of fans. You'll find one more interesting option just north of Reedsport in the **Gardiner Guest**

Giant rhododendrons and tumble-down shacks that rent out dune buggies and ATVs line US-101 between Florence and Coos Bay. Dune buggy tours ranging from peaceful to exhilarating are offered by **Sandland Adventures** (541/997-8087), less than a mile south of Florence's Siuslaw River Bridge.

House (401 Front St.; 541/543-0210), which offers comfortable B&B rooms in a restored Victorian home.

Perhaps the best introduction to the bewildering geography of the dunes region is **Umpqua Dunes,** nine miles south of the Reedsport visitors center. Another popular walk starts from Eel Creek Campground, heading for just under three miles across small marshes and conifer groves en route to the sea, negotiating lunar-like dunes soaring 300–500 feet—some of the tallest in the world. Another nice trek leaves from **Tahkenitch Lake,** a popular largemouth bass fishing spot north of Gardiner, and gives a more in-depth look at the dunes' diverse flora and fauna, including swans and (very rarely!) black bears.

> Fans of Frank Herbert's ecological sci-fi saga *Dune* may already know that the stories were inspired by the Oregon Dunes, south of Florence.

Coos Bay

Even if you race right through, it's quite apparent that **Coos Bay** (pop. 15,967), once the world's largest lumber port, retains a core of heavy industry. Many of the big mills have closed, and one has been replaced by **The Mill Casino,** a resort complex operated by native Coquille Indian tribe, but you can still watch huge piles of wood chips, the harbor's number-one export, being loaded onto factory ships in the harbor east of US-101. The chips are sent to Asia, where they're turned into paper. (One chip-ship that didn't make it into the harbor, the 640-foot-long *New Carissa,* wrecked in a 1999 storm and sat on the Coos Bay beach for years.)

> Behind the Coos Bay visitors bureau, a monument remembers the region's favorite son, middle- and long-distance runner Steve Prefontaine, who electrified the athletic world before his death in a 1975 car wreck, at the age of 24. An annual 10K memorial run is held in September.

There's very good seafood and other meals available at **Shark Bites** (240 S. Broadway; 541/269-7475), on US-101, while microbrews are served at the **Blue Heron Bistro** (100 Commercial Ave.; 541/267-3933), across from the visitors bureau. There's no shortage of easy-to-find lodging, including **Motel 6** ($45 and up; 1445 Bayshore Dr.; 541/267-7171) on US-101.

Shore Acres State Park

The historical antecedents for Coos Bay port development were laid a century ago by the Simpson Lumber Company, whose ships transported Oregon logs around the world. The ships returned

Nine miles west of Coos Bay, in the busy commercial and sport-fishing port of **Charleston,** you'll be welcomed to town by an unlikely sight: a flipper-waving statue of 1960s-era advertising icon Charlie the Tuna (of StarKist seafood fame).

with exotic seeds that were planted in the Simpson estate's garden, 12 miles west of Coos Bay via the Cape Arago Highway. Though the Simpson house burned to the ground in 1921, the five acres of formal gardens are still a floral fantasia, now open to the public as **Shore Acres State Park** (daily 8 AM–dusk). Besides the formal gardens, which are illuminated during the Christmas holiday season, there's an observation tower above wave-battered bluffs and a trail down to a delightful beach.

On the way to Shore Acres from Coos Bay is **Sunset Bay State Park,** perhaps Oregon's best swimming beach. South of Shore Acres is **Cape Arago State Park,** complete with tidepools and seals (and seal pups in springtime) lounging on offshore rocks. Mostly level trails lead along the coastline from Shore Acres to Sunset Bay and Cape Arago State Parks, and if you're tempted to stay overnight and explore the lovely region, consider taking advantage of one of Oregon's best-kept secrets: the roomy, tent-like **yurts** available for overnight rental (around $40; 800/452-5687) at Sunset Bay and in a dozen other state park beauty spots.

Bandon

There's no sharper contrast on the Oregon coast than the difference between industrial Coos Bay and earthy **Bandon** (pop. 3,066), 24 miles to the south. Here, in the **Old Town** section along the banks of the Coquille River, are several blocks of galleries, crafts shops, and fine restaurants, marked by a gateway arch off US-101. Start a tour of Old Town at the corner of 1st and Baltimore, where Big Wheel General Store houses the **Bandon Driftwood Museum** (daily; free), which gives a good sense of Bandon's back-to-the-land, hippie ethos. A more academic introduction to the town and region can be had at the **Bandon Historical Society Museum** (Mon.–Sat., daily in summer; $2; 270 Fillmore Ave.; 541/347-2164), in the old City Hall along US-101. Its exhibits on area history, cranberries, and local color are artfully done, and the

FACE ROCK, CAT AND KITTENS, BANDON BEACH

PHOTO BY WESLEY HEDDENS

building is easy to find, so be sure to stop. South of town, **Beach Loop Drive** runs along a ridge overlooking a fantastic assemblage of coastal monoliths.

For fish-and-chips along the waterfront, the **Bandon Fish Market** (249 1st St. SE; 541/347-4282) is cheap, cheerful, and very very good; a block to the east, looking more like a tackle shop than a restaurant, **Tony's Crab Shack** (541/347-2875) is another local landmark, famous for fish tacos, chowders, and silky crab sandwiches.

Bandon Beach

Outside of town, the exclusive and expensive (but open to the public) **Bandon Dunes Golf Resort** ($100 and up; 541/347-4380 or 888/345-6008) has been drawing raves from golfers, well-heeled vacationers, and landscape architects alike. Designed to preserve and enhance the "natural" scenery in the style of Scottish "links" courses rather than the anodyne green swaths that characterize most suburban country club courses, Bandon Dunes offers golf ($75–225 per round for resort guests), select accommodations, and a nice restaurant.

South of Bandon, 9.5 miles north of Port Orford, **Cape Blanco** is considered—by Oregonians, at least—the westernmost point of land in the contiguous United States. Named by early Spanish explorers for the white shells encrusting the 245-foot cliff face, the cape is also the site of Oregon's oldest (circa-1870) and highest lighthouse. The headland offers great views, and its windswept exposure draws pilots of radio-controlled model planes and gliders. If you need to warm your innards afterwards, stop in at the straightforward **Greasy Spoon Café** (541/348-2514) on US-101 in nearby Langlois for a cup of coffee and some classic biscuits-and-gravy.

Port Orford and Humbug Mountain

Pastoral sheep ranches, cranberry bogs, berry fields, and Christmas tree farms dominate the 25-mile stretch south of Bandon, but as you pull into **Port Orford** (pop. 1,133), you can't help but notice a huge volcanic plug abutting the crescent-shaped shoreline. Known as **Battle Rock,** in memory of a battle (re-enacted every 4th of July) in which early settlers fought off a party of hostile Indians, the rock is impressive from the harbor below, while a trail climbs up to the windblown summit. Due to the southwest orientation, which subjects the harbor to turbulent winds and constant waves, fishing boats have to be lowered into the water by crane, but surfers (and kite-surfers and windsurfers) don't seem to mind.

People who keep track of these things say that tiny Port Orford is the "most westerly incorporated city in the continental United States." Others grant it the less-welcome title of "rainiest place on the Oregon coast."

A nice place to stay in Port Orford is the **Home by the Sea Bed and Breakfast** ($85–115; 444 Jackson St.; 541/332-2855 or 877/332-2855), within walking distance to town along yet another stunning stretch of Oregon coastline.

Six miles south of Port Orford you'll come to **Humbug Mountain State Park,** whose 1,756-foot elevation flanks the west side of the highway. It's one of the coast's highest peaks rising directly off the beach, and its steep contours and tree-covered slopes are best appreciated from the steep but well-maintained three-mile trail that climbs to the summit. The mountain's name may have been bestowed by prospectors who found that tales of gold deposits here were just "humbug"—but the views from the top are splendid.

Prehistoric Gardens

On the west side of the highway, midway between Port Orford and Gold Beach, you'll come across one of the Oregon coast's tackiest but most enduring and enjoyable tourist traps, the **Prehistoric Gardens** (daily; $10 adults; 541/332-4463). Standing out like a sore thumb on this otherwise unspoiled stretch of US-101, brightly colored, more or less life-sized dinosaur sculptures inhabit the evocatively lush green forest. Since 1953, when amateur paleontologist E. V. Nelson sculpted his first concrete *T. rex,* nearly two dozen more have been added to the forest menagerie.

Gold Beach

Gold Beach was named for the nuggets mined from the area's black sands during the mid-19th century, but despite its name this is one coastal town where the action is definitely *away* from the beach. The **Rogue River** defines the northern city limits and is the town's economic raison d'être. During salmon season, Gold Beach hotels and restaurants fill up with anglers, while **jetboat tours** of the wild river are also a draw. **Jerry's Rogue Jets** ($45 and up; 541/247-4571 or 800/451-3645), by the bridge at the north end of town, takes passengers upstream to the isolated hamlet of **Agness,** where a homespun mountain lodge serves family-style fried-chicken lunches and dinners (the food is not included in the price of the jet-boat ride). Other trips head farther upstream to the Rogue River rapids and the roadless wilderness areas of the **Siskiyou National Forest;** these cost $65–90.

The usual motel rooms are available along US-101, but for a more memorable visit, try the **Tu Tu' Tun Lodge** ($135 and up; 96550 North Bank Rogue; 541/247-6664 or 800/864-6357). Set on a hill above the Rogue River, seven miles upstream from the coast, this upscale fishing lodge (pronounced "ta-TWO-tun") has plushly rustic rooms and a great restaurant.

Southern Oregon's coastal forests yield the increasingly rare and disease-threatened Port Orford cedar, a very valuable (up to $50,000 per tree) and very fragrant wood popular for use in Japanese home construction.

Mt. Emily, just east of Brookings, was bombed by a submarine-launched Japanese seaplane in September 1942. Though the Japanese plans to ignite the entire coastline in a massive forest fire fizzled, the attack weakened a short-lived secession movement by southern Oregonians and northern Californians to establish a new state called Jefferson.

Samuel H. Boardman State Scenic Corridor

Between Gold Beach and Brookings, US-101's windy, hilly roadbed is studded with the cliffside ocean vistas, giant conifers, and boomerang-shaped offshore rock formations of **Samuel H. Boardman State Scenic Corridor.** The park covers 12 of the "Fabulous 50" miles between the two towns, and all of the features come together at Natural Bridges Cove. Located just north of the Thomas Creek Bridge (the highest bridge in Oregon), this turnout is easy to miss despite being well signed because, from the highway, it appears to be simply a parking lot fronting some trees. From the south end of the parking lot, however, a short trail through an old-growth forest leads to a viewpoint several hundred feet above three natural rock archways standing out from an azure cove.

Brookings: Harris Beach State Park

The drive through the malled-over main drag of **Brookings** offers only fleeting glimpses of the Pacific, and if you're hoping for a first or last "Wow!" before or after the 300-plus other miles of coastal Oregon's scenic splendor, these few miles along the California border may be somewhat anticlimactic. That said, Brookings does have beautiful Azalea Park (which is gorgeous during the April–June spring bloom). The popular, welcoming beachfront B&B rooms at **Lowden's Beachfront Bed & Breakfast,** on Wollam Road just west of US-101 ($109 and up; 541/469-7045) offer direct access to a driftwood-strewn beach.

Just north of Brookings, one final piece of Oregon's abundant natural beauty has been preserved at **Harris Beach State Park,** across US-101 from the Oregon Welcome Center. Here you can walk down to a driftwood-laden beach and look out at Bird Island, where rare birds breed.

Heading south, just over the California border from Brookings lies Redwood National Park, truly one of the West Coast's great places.

CALIFORNIA

Stretching along the Pacific Ocean for roughly a thousand miles from top to tail, the California coast includes virgin wilderness, the cutting edge of cosmopolitan culture, and the full spectrum in between. For almost the entire way, coastal roads give quick and easy access to the best parts, with panoramic views appearing so often you'll simply give up trying to capture it all.

Starting in the north, the green forests of the Pacific Northwest continue well beyond the state border, forming a mountainous seaside landscape that lasts until the edge of metropolitan **San Francisco.** Along this stretch you'll find a number of old logging and fishing towns, varying from the burly blue-collar likes of **Eureka** and **Crescent City** to the upscale ambience of **Mendocino,** in and amongst endless acres of redwood forest.

At the approximate midpoint of the California coast sits **San Francisco,** deservedly ranked among the world's favorite cities. The 100 miles of coast stretching south from San Francisco hold numerous remnants of the Spanish and Mexican eras, exemplified by the town of **Monterey** and the beautiful mission at

Carmel. Beyond here is another stretch of wild coastline, the rugged country of **Big Sur.**

Beyond the southern edge of Big Sur, opulent **Hearst Castle** marks the start of what most people consider Southern California, the rivers and trees of the north giving way to golden beaches, grassy bluffs, and considerably denser populations. A pair of very pleasant small cities, Midwestern-feeling **San Luis Obispo** and ritzy **Santa Barbara,** make excellent stops in themselves, smoothing the transition into the environs of **Los Angeles,** the unwieldy megalopolis that, seen from the I-5 freeway that links Los Angeles and **San Diego,** seems like one monstrous, 100-mile-long suburb. While it's true that the natural beauty that brought so many people to Southern California in the first place is increasingly endangered, some lovely, almost untouched places remain, hidden away but within easy access of the fast lane. We've pointed them out; enjoy them while they last.

Jedediah Smith Redwoods State Park

The northernmost of the great redwood groves, **Jedediah Smith Redwoods State Park** covers nearly 10,000 acres of virgin forest along the banks of the Smith River. Stretching east of US-101, and most easily accessible from US-199, the park offers over 20 miles of usually uncrowded hiking trails through the pristine wilderness; it is considered by many the most perfect of all the redwood forests. One of the most enjoyable trails leads through **Stout Grove,** past tall trees and a number of summertime swimming holes along the Smith River.

There's also a good **campground** (800/444-7275) with hot showers. For fans of roadside kitsch, there's one unique spot along US-101 in the hamlet of Smith River, 15 miles north of

The Smith River and Jedediah Smith Redwoods State Park were named in memory of the legendary mountain man Jedediah Strong Smith, who in 1826 at the age of 27 led the first party of Americans overland to California. Smith also blazed the first trail over South Pass through the Rocky Mountains, later used by the Oregon Trail pioneers.

Crescent City: **Ship Ashore** (707/487-3141), a gift shop, restaurant, campground and motel along US-101, marked by a grounded but still handsome 1920s yacht, inside which is a gift shop and seashell museum.

Crescent City

The county seat and only incorporated city in Del Norte County, **Crescent City** (pop. 8,805) is best treated as a base from which to explore the surrounding wilderness. The foggy weather that helps the redwoods thrive makes the city fairly depressing and gray, and what character it developed since its founding in the 1850s has been eroded by storms; a giant tsunami, caused by the 1964 earthquake off Alaska, destroyed much of the city. The more recent tsunami unleashed by the 2011 quake in Sendai, Japan, was less destructive but drowned one man and caused millions in damage to boats moored in the Crescent City harbor.

Outside Crescent City, California's most violent long-term criminals are kept behind bars in the state-of-the-art Pelican Bay State Prison, opened in 1989.

Crescent City includes the familiar lineup of motels and restaurants, plus local options like the **Beacon Burger** (160 Anchor Way; 707/464-6565), south of downtown. Sugar junkies will want to stop at the **Continental Bakery,** a great doughnut shop on US-101 (503 L St.; 707/465-5652). For overnight, one only-in-California option is the **Curly Redwood Lodge** ($56 and up; 701 S. Redwood Hwy./US-101 S. 707/464-2137), a nicely maintained 1950s motel made from a single, sawn-up redwood tree.

Del Norte Coast Redwoods State Park

Spreading south from the Jedediah Smith redwoods, **Del Norte Coast Redwoods State Park** runs along the Pacific Ocean (and US-101) for about eight miles, containing more than 6,000 acres of first- and second-growth redwoods as well as brilliant blooms of rhododendrons, azaleas, and spring wildflowers. Del Norte also protects miles of untouched coastline, the best stretch of which is accessible from the end of **Enderts Beach Road,** which cuts west from US-101 just north of the park entrance. From here, a 30-mile trail follows the coast to Prairie Creek. The state park area is bounded on the south by an undeveloped section of **Redwood National Park.**

Trees of Mystery and Klamath

Hard to miss along US-101, thanks to the massive statues of Paul Bunyan and Babe the Blue Ox looming over the highway, the

Trees of Mystery (hours vary; $14; 707/482-2251) are literally and figuratively the biggest tourist draws on the Northern California coast. Along the Trail of Tall Tales, chainsaw-cut figures, backed by audio-taped stories, stand in tableaux at the foot of towering redwoods. There's also a SkyTrail gondola lifting passengers up into the treetop canopy, a huge gift shop, and a small free museum of Native American art and artifacts. Across the highway, **Motel Trees** (707/482-3152) has standard rooms (from $75) and a café.

Along the banks of the mighty Klamath River, four miles south of the Trees of Mystery, the town of **Klamath** (pop. 779) is a brief burst of highway sprawl, supported by anglers who flock here for the annual fall salmon runs—provided there are any fish left to catch. Fisherfolk, walkers, and kayakers all avail themselves of the enduringly popular **The Historic Requa Inn** ($89 and up; 866/800-8777), a friendly and very comfortable nearly century-old homestead right on the riverfront. At the south end of

All the land along the Klamath River is part of the extensive **Hoopa Valley Indian Reservation,** which stretches for over 30 miles upstream from the Pacific Ocean.

Klamath town, take a drive right through the **Tour-Thru Tree** ($5), then cross the Klamath River on a bridge graced by a pair of gilded cement grizzly bears.

Prairie Creek Redwoods State Park

The largest of the trio of north coast state redwood parks, **Prairie Creek Redwoods State Park** is best known for its large herd of endangered Roosevelt elk, which you can usually see grazing in the meadows along US-101 at the center of the park, next to the main ranger station (707/465-7347). A modern freeway carries US-101 traffic around, rather than through, the Prairie Creek redwoods, so to reach the best sights, detour along the well-signed Newton B. Drury Scenic Parkway, which follows Prairie Creek along the old US-101 alignment through the heart of the park.

Another elk herd can be spotted among the coastal dunes at **Gold Bluffs Beach,** which stretches for 11 miles through un-touched wilderness; there are trails leading from US-101, or you can follow Davison Road northwest from US-101, three miles south of the ranger station. Apart from the elk, Prairie Creek offers the usual mix of old-growth redwood trees, which here, more than in the other parks, mingle with dense growths of Sitka spruce and Douglas firs to form a near rainforest of greenery.

Redwood National Park

Established in 1968, and enlarged since then, **Redwood National Park** protects the last vestiges of the more than two million acres of primeval redwood forest that once covered the entire Northern California coastline. To be honest, alongside the gor-geous groves in the adjacent Smith, Del Norte, and Prairie Creek State Parks, the trees preserved here aren't by any means the old-est, largest, or most beautiful. In fact, much of the federal park-land is second- or third-growth timber, clear-cut as recently as the 1960s. Though redwoods are the fastest-growing softwoods on earth—growing 3–5 feet a year when young—the groves here

can look rather disap-pointing compared to those in nearby areas, but they do serve a valuable role as an en-vironmental buffer zone even if they're not exactly a tree-lover's pilgrimage site.

That said, Redwood National Park does hold two special sights, including the **Lady Bird Johnson Grove,** on Bald Hill Road two miles east of US-101, where the new park was dedicated in 1969. Ten miles farther up this road, and a long hike beyond that, the Tall Trees Grove (free permit required) holds one of the world's tallest trees, the 360-plus-foot Libbey Tree, whose trunk measures over 14 feet in diameter.

> The groves of giant trees in Redwood National Park were used as a location for the Star Wars film *Return of the Jedi,* in which the characters cruised through the forest on airborne cycles. Patrick's Point played a starring role in the sequel to *Jurassic Park.*

At the south end of the park, the roadside-strip town of **Orick** stretches toward the coast, where the main Redwood National Park **visitors center** (707/465-7765) stands at the mouth of Redwood Creek.

Patrick's Point State Park

If your idea of heaven is sitting on a rocky headland listening to the roar of the Pacific while watching the sunset or looking for passing gray whales, you won't want to pass by **Patrick's Point State Park** (707/677-3570). Three different 200-foot-high promontories at the heart of the park provide panoramic views, while the surrounding acres hold cedar and spruce forests (no redwoods), open pastures bright with wildflowers, great tidepools, a wide dark-sand beach, and two campgrounds (800/444-7275) with hot showers. There's also the preserved and restored remnants of a Yurok village, a redwood dugout canoe, and a garden of traditional herbs.

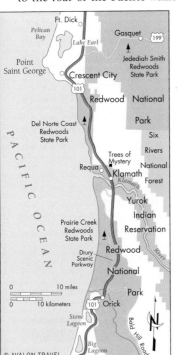

Continuing south, US-101 becomes a four-lane freeway along the ocean to Arcata and Eureka, but most of the old US-101 alignment

The author Bret Harte was run out of Arcata by angry townspeople in 1860, after writing an editorial in the local paper criticizing a massacre of a local Wiyot tribe.

PLEASE
DO NOT CLIMB
ON ROCKS

Inland from Arcata along scenic US-299, the town of **Willow Creek** claims to be the heart of Bigfoot Country, boasting a large statue of the furry beast to prove it. One of the state's most scenic drives (or bike rides), US-299 continues east over the coast range through the beautiful Trinity Alps to Weaverville, well-preserved site of a mid-1850s gold rush, before linking up with I-5 at Redding.

winds along the cliff tops between Patrick's Point and the small town of Trinidad. Along this road you'll find some places to stay, like the **Trinidad Inn** ($75 and up; 1170 Patrick's Point Dr.; 707/677-3349), about three miles south of the park entrance. A little farther down this old stretch of US-101 is **The Larrupin' Cafe** (closed Wed.; 1658 Patrick's Point Dr.; 707/677-0230), which serves up bountiful portions of very fresh all-American food in a friendly, homey ambience—it's California cuisine without the snooty pretense you sometimes find farther south.

Arcata

The most attractive and enjoyable town on the far north coast of California, **Arcata** (pop. 15,700) makes the best first (or last, depending upon the direction you're traveling) overnight stop south of the Oregon border. The presence of Humboldt State University's campus on the hills above US-101 accounts for the town's youthful, nonconformist energy. Cafés, bookstores, bars, and crafts shops surround the lively **Arcata Plaza,** two blocks west of US-101 at 9th and G Streets, incongruously graced by palm trees and a statue of President McKinley. The *Utne Reader* once rated Arcata as the most enlightened town in California, and spending even a little time in this vibrant, cooperative Ecotopia may make you wonder whether or not you really do have to race back to the big-city 9-to-5 grind.

You can admire the town's many elaborate Victorian-era cottages, hunt wild mushrooms, clamber over sand dunes, or hike in the redwoods; afterward, relax with a cup of tea or, better yet, a soak in a hot tub at homey **Cafe Mokka,** the coast's only combo sauna and espresso bar, at 5th and J Streets (707/822-2228). Just off the plaza, **Jambalaya** (915 H St.; 707/822-4766) serves burgers, sandwiches, and (of course) jambalaya, while microbrews flow from the taps of Arcata's amiable bars, many of which feature live music. For food, drink, and entertainment all under one roof, head to the very popular "HumBrews," a.k.a. the **Humboldt Brews** (856 10th St.; 707/826-2739). For a complete selection of foodstuffs and supplies, and more insight into the local community, head to the large and stylish **North Coast Co-op** (811 I St.), a block west from the plaza.

For a place to stay, the centrally located **Hotel Arcata** ($85 and up; 708 9th St.; 707/826-0217 or 800/344-1221) is right on the plaza, or you can take your pick of the usual motels along US-101.

Eureka

Evolving into a lively artists' colony from its roots as a fairly gritty and industrial port, **Eureka** (pop. 28,606) was well known to fur-trappers and traders long before it became a booming lumber and whaling port in the 1850s. Thanks to the lumber trade, Victorian Eureka grew prosperous, building elaborate homes, including the oft-photographed but closed to the public **Carson Mansion** along the waterfront at 2nd and M Streets, two blocks west of US-101.

Along with dozens of well-preserved Victorian houses, Eureka has done a fine job of finding new uses for its many ornate commercial buildings, most of which have been preserved to house art galleries, cafés, and restaurants in what's now called **Old Town,** a half dozen blocks between the waterfront and US-101. This historic down-

One unique thing to see in Eureka is the **Romano Gabriel Wooden Sculpture Garden** (315 2nd St.), displayed in a plate-glass showcase. This brilliantly colorful folk-art extravaganza of faces and flowers originally stood in the front yard of local gardener Romano Gabriel, who made them out of discarded packing crates and other recycled materials over a period of some 30 years before his death in 1977.

Kinetic Grand Championship

Humboldt County's creative community comes alive every Memorial Day weekend for the world-famous Kinetic Grand Championship, in which participants pedal, paddle, and otherwise move themselves and their handmade vehicles across land and sea. Part art, part engineering, and part athletic competition, the Kinetic Grand Championship is like nothing you've seen before. Also known as the "Kinetic Sculpture Race" and "The Triathlon of the Art World," the event begins midday Saturday and runs until Monday afternoon, as a mind-boggling array of mobile contraptions—past winners have included everything from dragons and floating flying saucers to Egyptian pyramids (named Queen of Denial) and a Cadillac Coupe de Ville—make their way over land, sand, and sea from the town square of Arcata to the main street of Ferndale, twice crossing chilly Humboldt Bay.

Rule Number One of the Kinetic Grand Championship is that all of the "sculptures" must be people-powered; beyond that, imagination is

"Just for the Halibut": racing along Samoa Peninsula

town quarter has a huge number of good places to eat and drink, including **Ramone's Bakery & Cafe** (209 E St.; 707/445-2923), the pub-like **Cafe Waterfront** (102 F St.; 707/443-9190), and the popular **Sea Grill** (316 E St.; 707/443-7187), a block from US-101. And if that's not enough to sate your appetite, for fish-and-chips and a pint or two of ale head along to the **Lost Coast Brewery** (617 4th St.; 707/445-4480).

Accommodation options range from roadside motels to upscale places like the **Carter House Inns** ($159 and up; 301 L St.; 707/444-8062), a re-created Victorian manor with spacious rooms and a big breakfast in the morning. For a more authentic Victorian experience, stay at one of California's most delightful B&Bs, the **Elegant Victorian Mansion** ($135 and up; 1406 C St.; 707/444-3144). A real treasure in a land of nice B&Bs, this magnificently restored 1888 Eastlake-style home has the primary guide. Many "rules" have developed over the years since the race was first run in 1969, including such pearls as: "In the Event of Sunshine, the Race Shall Proceed," but most of these emphasize the idea that maintaining style and a sense of humor are at least as important as finishing the fastest. Since the Grand Prizes are valued at somewhere around $14.98, racers take part solely for the glory, but prizes are awarded in many categories: First- and last-place finishers are winners, and the racer who finishes in the exact middle of the pack gets the coveted Mediocre Award—historically a broken-down old banger.

Spectators are expected to be active participants, too, so be prepared to shout and scream and applaud the competitors, or even jog or bike or kayak alongside them. There are many great vantage points along the route, but you have to be in the right place on the right day. Before noon on Saturday there's a pre-race lineup around Arcata Plaza, from where racers head through the streets of Arcata out toward the Manila Dunes before spending the first night in downtown Eureka. Sunday morning the racers head across Humboldt Bay from Field's Landing, then camp out overnight on the beach. Monday's trials include another water crossing, and it all culminates in a mad dash down the Main Street of Ferndale, surrounded by cheering multitudes. It's all good fun, and a great focus for a visit to this remarkable corner of the world.

been opulently decorated with real antiques and Bradbury & Bradbury wallpapers by the hospitable Belgian-born innkeeper, Lily Vieyra.

For further information, about Eureka or anywhere in the whole glorious Redwood Empire region, contact the **Humboldt County Convention and Visitors Bureau** (1034 2nd St.; 707/443-5097 or 800/346-3482).

Samoa

Even if you're just passing through, don't miss the chance to visit the old mill town of **Samoa,** across the bay from Eureka but easily reachable via the Hwy-255 bridge. Here on a narrow peninsula between the bay and the open ocean, the unique **Samoa Cookhouse** (707/442-1659) was built in 1890 to feed the many hungry men living and working in the "company town" lumber mill here. The mill is long gone now, but the cookhouse remains in operation as a sort of living history center, packed with logging memorabilia and blue-collar character. So take a seat at one of the 20-foot-long tables (redwood, of course, covered in checkered oilcloth), soak up the history, and dig into the family-style feasts (breakfast, lunch, and dinner daily—all-you-can-eat!). There are no menus, just huge platters of food at very reasonable prices.

Ferndale

Well worth the 10-mile round-trip detour west of US-101, the historic town of **Ferndale** (pop. 1,371) is an odd fish along the woodsy Northern California coast, a century-old dairy town that would look more at home in middle America. The three-block-long, franchise-free Main Street includes a fully stocked general store, the **Golden Gait Mercantile** (421 Main St.), and whitewashed farmhouses dot the pastoral valleys nearby. Ferndale's diverse history is well documented inside the **Ferndale Art & Cultural Center** (hours vary; 580 Main St.; 707/786-4466), where some of the wacky racers that take part in the annual **Kinetic Grand Championship** are displayed.

Ambling along Main Street is the best way to get a feel for Ferndale, and if you build up an appetite, there are many good places to eat. One of the oldest cafés in the West, **Poppa Joe's** (409 Main St.; 707/786-4180), serves great diner food in a no-frills Victorian-era storefront, while one of California's earliest hotels features a family-friendly Italian restaurant, **The Hotel Ivanhoe Restaurant &**

Saloon (315 Main St.; 707/786-9000), open for dinner only. On the main road midway between town and US-101 is another fast-foodie landmark: the **No Brand Burger Stand** (1400 Main St.; 707/786-9474), where all the tasty patties are hand-formed from local grass-fed beef. Fab fries and luscious milk shakes, too. Yum.

The area around Ferndale has been hit by numerous earthquakes, including a destructive tremor in April 1992 that registered 7.2 on the Richter scale.

Along with its good food options, Ferndale is equally well supplied with places to stay. Right off the heart of Main Street is the clean and tidy **Redwood Suites** ($95 and up; 332 Ocean Ave.; 707/786-5000). Also nice is **The Shaw House Inn** ($125 and up; 703 Main St.; 707/786-9958), an 1854 American Gothic masterpiece with B&B rooms for rent.

The Lost Coast

Between Ferndale and Rockport, the main US-101 highway heads inland along the Eel River, but if you have time and a taste for adventure, head west from Ferndale along the narrow, winding Mattole Road, which loops around Cape Mendocino through the northern reaches of the so-called **Lost Coast,** a 100-mile stretch of shoreline justly famous for its isolated beauty. By road, you can only get close to the ocean at a few points—the few miles south of Cape Mendocino, and again at the fishing resort of **Shelter Cove,** west of Garberville—but hikers can have a field day (or week) exploring the extensive coastal wilderness. Some 50 miles of rugged, untouched coastline, packed with tidepools and driftwood-strewn beaches, have been preserved in a pair of parks, the **King Range National Conservation Area** in the north and the **Sinkyone Wilderness State Park** farther south.

The Lost Coast area was the site of the first oil well in California, which was drilled in the 1860s in the town of **Petrolia** but is now long gone.

Besides the Hwy-211/Mattole Road, which makes a 70-mile loop between Ferndale and the Rockefeller Forest section of Humboldt Redwoods State Park, a network of rougher and even more remote routes allows auto access to the Lost Coast, linking the hamlet of Honeydew with coastal Hwy-1 near Rockport. If you do explore this wild (and very rainy) region, take a good map and plenty of food and water, and be careful.

For further information on the Lost Coast, contact the **Bureau of Land Management** (1695 Heindon Rd.; 707/825-2300); its office is off US-101 on the north side of Arcata.

Scotia

Back along US-101, on the banks of the Eel River midway between the coast and the Humboldt Redwoods, **Scotia** was the last true company town left in California. The Pacific Lumber Company (a.k.a. PALCO) built it and for most of the 20th century owned and operated everything, from the two huge wood-cutting mills to the 10 blocks of pastel-painted houses, church, and schools that constituted this little community of about 1,000 people.

The lumber mills used to be the heart and soul of the town, as well as Scotia's main tourist attraction, but after a 1980s junk-bond leveraged buyout and subsequent asset-stripping PALCO finally went bankrupt in 2007. Since then the town and the mills have struggled to find a way forward, but Scotia is still a proud and photogenic place, well worth a look and a wander.

In summer, the heart of Scotia is the rustic and historic **Winema Theater,** which screens movies on weekend nights

(plus an old-fashioned Saturday matinee). The one place to stay in town is the rustic **Scotia Inn** ($75 and up; 100 Main St.; 707/764-5338), which has B&B rooms and a very good restaurant. Part of the old lumber mill has been reconfigured into a biofueled home for the excellent (and 100 percent organic) **Eel River Brewery,** which operates a popular tasting room and restaurant at its original location near Ferndale, off US-101 in the hamlet of Fortuna (1777 Alamar Way; 707/725-2739).

Humboldt Redwoods State Park

Sheltering the biggest and best collection of giant coastal redwoods anywhere in the world, **Humboldt Redwoods State**

Park is an exceptionally breathtaking corner of an exceptionally beautiful region. Covering more than 53,000 acres along the Eel River, this is the true heart of redwood country, containing the largest and most pristine expanses of virgin forest as well as some of the largest, tallest, and most remarkable trees.

The protection of the mighty redwood forests of Northern California was made possible not by the state or federal governments but primarily by the efforts of the **Save the Redwoods League,** a private organization that has raised, since its founding in 1918, millions of dollars to buy or preserve over 185,000 acres of redwood forest. To support these efforts, write to 114 Sansome Street, Suite 1200, San Francisco, CA 94104, or call 415/362-2352.

Even if you're just passing through, be sure to turn onto the amazing **Avenue of the Giants,** 31 miles of old highway frontage between Pepperwood and Phillipsville. This sinuous old road snakes alongside, and sometimes under, the faster and busier US-101 freeway, which is carried on concrete stilts through the park. In and amongst the natural wonders along the Avenue of the Giants are a handful of man-made ones: The **Eternal Tree House** in Redcrest and the **Shrine Drive-Thru Tree** in Myers Flat are just two of the many good-natured "tourist traps" in this neck of the woods. At the north end of the park you'll find an impressive collection of trees in the well-marked **Founder's Grove,** where a half-mile nature trail leads past the 362-foot-tall, possibly 2,000-year-old **Dyerville Giant,** lauded as one of the world's tallest trees before it fell during the winter of 1991.

Once you've done the Avenue of the Giants, if you want to escape the crowds and the freeway rumble, head west from Founder's Grove across US-101, to the 10,000-plus-acre **Rockefeller Forest.** This expansive grove is one of the largest old-growth forests in the world and includes two of the world's champion trees, each over 360 feet tall and some 17 feet in diameter.

The best source of information on the park is the **visitors center** (707/946-2263), midway along the Avenue of the Giants in Weott; there's a pleasant state-run **campground** (800/444-7275) with showers right next door. You may have to drive a ways north (to Ferndale, Eureka, or Arcata) or south (to Garberville) from the park to find an exceptional meal, though there are a few nice places to stay, like the historic **Myers Country Inn** ($180 and up; 707/943-3259), midway along the

Avenue of the Giants in Myers Flat. Farther south, the hamlet of Miranda holds the pleasant **Miranda Gardens Resort** ($105 and up; 707/943-3011), with rustic cabins.

Garberville and Redway

Apart from its recurring presence in the national media during the occasional high-profile raids on local marijuana plantations, the redwood country town of **Garberville** is a pretty quiet, peaceful place. The US-101 freeway bypasses the town, and locals walk and talk to each other along the half dozen blocks of Redwood Drive, the well-signed business loop off the highway.

Enjoy an early-morning breakfast with the old-time locals at the **Eel River Cafe** (801 Redwood Dr.; 707/923-3783), or an espresso and healthy food at the **Woodrose Café,** a block south (911 Redwood Dr.; 707/923-3191). Garberville also has all the motels you could want, including the **Motel Garberville** ($50 and up; 948 Redwood Dr.; 707/923-2422).

The Reggae on the River festival, organized by the energetic Mateel Community Center (707/923-3368), attracts world-class performers and thousands of fans every July.

Two miles west of Garberville on the old highway, **Redway** is worth the short side trip for an organic burger at **Deb's Great American Hamburgers** (707/923-2244), or a slice of pizza or fine dinner at **The Mateel Cafe** (707/923-2030), a health-conscious gourmet haunt at the center of town.

The Garberville/Redway area is home to a pretty unusual community of old hippies and off-the-grid libertarians, who share their music and politics on noncommercial local radio station **KMUD 91.1 FM.**

Along US-101, four miles south of Garberville, one of the region's most characterful places is the stately **Benbow Hotel & Resort** ($100–200; 707/923-2124), a circa-1926 mock Tudor hotel with a nice restaurant offering afternoon tea and scones on a sunny terrace overlooking Lake Benbow.

Leggett: The Chandelier Drive-Thru Tree

No longer even a proverbial wide spot in the road since the US-101 freeway was diverted around it, **Leggett** marks the southern end of the Humboldt redwoods. At the south end of "town," a mile from the US-101/Hwy-1 junction along the old highway, stands one of the redwood region's most venerable and worthwhile roadside attractions, the "original" **Chandelier Drive-Thru Tree**

Avenue of the Giants

The stretch of historic US-101 through the redwood country of Humboldt County, frequently called the "Avenue of the Giants," is lined by pristine groves of massive trees and provides boundless opportunities to come face-to-face with your own insignificance in nature's greater scheme of things. If you tire of this display of natural majesty, or simply want to keep it in context with the modern "civilized" world, you're in luck: Every few miles, amongst the stately trees, you'll come upon shameless souvenir stands selling redwood burl furniture and chainsaw sculptures, as well as wonderfully tacky tourist traps like the Legend of Bigfoot. Many of these hyper-tacky attractions now exist only in memory (and on old postcards!), but none of

the survivors is big or bold enough to detract from the main event—the big trees—and since they've been in operation since the early days of car-borne tourism, they're as much a part of the redwood experience as the trees themselves. Most charge only a few dollars' admission, so there's not a lot to lose.

at the end of Leggett, the "original" Drive-Thru Tree

While you're encouraged to stop at any and all of them—at least long enough to buy a postcard or two—the most tried-and-true attraction is the **Trees of Mystery,** marked by huge statues of Paul Bunyan and Babe the Blue Ox along US-101 in Klamath, well north of the official Avenue of the Giants. In Myers Flat is the **Shrine Drive-Thru Tree,** at 13078 Avenue of the Giants (old US-101), which wagon-borne travelers drove through more than a century ago. Two more classics are found in the south: One of the best stops in redwood country, **Confusion Hill** in Piercy is one of those places where water runs uphill and the rules of physics seem not to apply, and there's also a little railway train here that chugs uphill to a very nice grove of trees. Finally, at the **Chandelier Drive-Thru Tree,** in Leggett off old US-101 on Drive Thru Tree Road, drive your car through a 315-foot redwood tree, still growing strong despite the gaping hole in its belly.

(daily dawn–dusk; $5). In addition to the famous tree, which had the six-foot-nine-inch-tall tunnel cut through it in the 1930s, there's an above-average gift shop with a broad range of books, postcards, and covetably schlocky souvenirs.

Nearby, the 16-acre grounds of **Big Bend Lodge** (summer only, $125 and up; 707/925-2440) has nine very quaint river-front cabins, perfect for lazy days floating, swimming, or fishing. South of Leggett, US-101 runs inland racing toward San Francisco, while scenic Hwy-1 cuts west over the coastal mountains to Mendocino, winding slowly south along the Pacific.

Rockport and Westport

From US-101 at Leggett, Hwy-1 twists up and over the rugged coastal mountains before hugging the coast through the weatherbeaten logging and fishing communities of **Rockport** and **Westport.** The small and informal **Howard Creek Ranch Inn** ($90 and up; 707/964-6725) in Westport offers comfortable B&B rooms, an outdoor hot tub, and easy access to the driftwood-laden beach. (But be warned: It's a half-hour drive to the nearest restaurants, in Fort Bragg.) Farther south, **MacKerricher State Park** protects seven miles of rocky coast and waterfront pine forest; there's also a nice campground (800/444-7275). An old logging railroad right-of-way, called Ten-Mile Haul Road, has been brought back into use as a hiking and cycling path that covers most of the eight miles between the north end of MacKerricher and the town Fort Bragg, crossing over Pudding Creek on a recently renovated railroad trestle.

Fort Bragg

Cruising south along Hwy-1, 40 miles from Leggett and US-101, the first real town you come to is **Fort Bragg** (pop. 6,963), whose burly, blue-collar edge comes as something of a shock on the otherwise undeveloped, touristy Mendocino coast. Formerly home to a large Georgia-Pacific lumber mill (plans to redevelop it are still in the works and may include eco-friendly housing and a shopping and light industrial complex), and still home to the region's largest commercial fishing fleet, Fort Bragg takes a mostly no-frills approach to the tourist trade, leaving the dainty B&B scene to

From Fort Bragg, the **California Western** railroad runs a number of historic steam- and diesel-powered Skunk Trains over the mountains to Willits and back. Half-day and full-day trips ($34–119; 866/457-5865) run year-round.

its upscale neighbor, Mendocino. However, the coastline is lovely, and there are a few down-to-earth places to eat, starting with the very good omelets and other eggy dishes at the appropriately named **Egghead's Restaurant** (326 N. Main St.; 707/964-5005). Perhaps the most popular place in town is **North Coast Brewing Co.** (455 N. Main St.; 707/964-2739), which serves good food and fine pints of its tasty Red Seal Ale among at least a dozen top-notch brews. As you might expect, Fort Bragg has a number of time-worn bars and taverns, like the **Golden West Saloon** (128 E. Redwood Ave.), two blocks south of the brewery.

Fort Bragg also boasts some unexpected treats: great hot dogs at **Relish** (260 N. Main St.; 707/962-0633), next door to the local legend that is **Cowlick's Ice Cream Café,** and the best pizza for miles, at **D'Aurelios,** a block east of Hwy-1 (438 S. Franklin St.; 707/964-4227).

Fort Bragg also has at least one exemplar of that rare species, the inexpensive (by Mendocino coast standards, at least) motel: the **Beachcomber Motel** ($99 and up; 1111 N. Main St.; 707/964-2402). Handy for the Ten-Mile Haul Road path, this is pretty much the coast's only beachfront accommodation option (apart from camping).

aerial view of Fort Bragg

At the south edge of Fort Bragg, near the Hwy-20 junction and eight miles north of the town of Mendocino, 47 acres of intensely landscaped coastal hillsides tumble down between Hwy-1 and the ocean to form the **Mendocino Coast Botanical Gardens** (daily; $14; 707/964-4352), a nonprofit public space showing off the abundance of plant life that thrives in this mild, lush environment. Cultivated varieties like camellias, azaleas, roses, irises, fuchsias, and dahlias share space with native ferns, pines, redwoods, wildflowers, and wetland plants. It's also the only public garden in the continental USA that fronts right onto the ocean, so you can enjoy crashing waves and maybe even watch a gray whale spout offshore.

Mendocino

One of the prettiest towns on the California coast (as seen in TV shows like *Murder, She Wrote* and numerous movies), **Mendocino** (pop. 894) is an artists' and writers' community par excel-

Mendocino

lence. Now firmly established as an upscale escape for wage-slaving visitors from San Francisco (hence the local nickname, "Spendocino"), the town was originally established as a logging port in the 1850s. In recent years, Mendocino has successfully preserved its rugged sandstone coastline—great for wintertime whale-watching—while converting many of its New England–style clapboard houses into super-quaint B&B inns. The area is ideal for leisurely wandering, following the many paths winding through **Mendocino Headlands State Park,** which wraps around the town and offers uninterrupted views across open fields, heathers, and other coastal flora to the crashing ocean beyond. For field guides, maps, or a look at Mendocino in its lumbering heyday, stop by the **visitors center** (707/937-5804) in the historic **Ford House** (735 Main St.).

Two miles north of town, one of the north coast's most perfect places is protected as **Russian Gulch State Park** (707/937-5804), where a waterfall, a soaring highway bridge, lush inland canyons, a swimming beach, and a impressive blow-hole are yours to enjoy along more than a mile of undisturbed coastline. There's camping, too, and sea kayaking, plus a fairly flat, three-mile paved bike trail and miles of hiking.

Along with its many fine art galleries and bookshops, the town of Mendocino also has a delicious collection of bakeries, cafés, and restaurants. If you're not getting a breakfast at a B&B, come to the very friendly **Mendocino Cafe** (10451 Lansing St.; 707/937-6141), where locals have been starting their days for more than 20 years. Lunch or dinner at **The Moosse Café** (390 Kasten St.; 707/937-4323) is always unforgettable. For a total splurge, try one of California's most famous (and expensive!) restaurants, **Cafe Beaujolais** (961 Ukiah St.; 707/937-5614), two blocks from the waterfront, which serves California cuisine delicacies for dinner nightly starting at 5:30 PM and for lunch Wednesday–Sunday.

Places to stay in Mendocino are rather expensive but generally delightful. The lovely **MacCallum House Inn** ($150 and up; 45020 Albion St.; 707/937-0289) includes a beautiful garden, good breakfasts, and a cozy nighttime bar and restaurant. Another place to stay is the circa-1858 **Mendocino Hotel & Garden Suites** ($129 and up; 45080 Main St.; 707/937-0511), on the downtown waterfront.

Mendocino, as you might expect from a well-heeled artists colony, also has a pretty lively music scene. **Dick's Place** is at the west end of Main Street (707/937-6010), and another long-standing local landmark draws familiar names from all over the world: **The Caspar Inn,** a historic roadhouse nightclub three miles north of town, just past Russian Gulch State Park and just west of Hwy-1 (707/964-5565).

Van Damme State Park

Three miles south of Mendocino at the mouth of the Little River, **Van Damme State Park** stretches along the coastal bluffs and beaches and includes some 1,800 acres of pine and redwood forest. The park's unique attribute is the oddly contorted **Pygmy Forest,** a natural bonsai-like grove of miniature pines, cypress, and manzanita, with a wheelchair-accessible nature trail explaining the unique ecology. There's also a small, very popular campground, concession-guided ocean kayak tours, and a **visitors center** (707/937-0851) housed in a New Deal–era recreation hall.

The nearby hamlet of Little River is home to some rural-feeling, peaceful alternatives to Mendocino's in-town accommodations: the very comfy **The Inn at Schoolhouse Creek** ($140 and up; 800/731-5525), where quaint cottages sit in nine acres of dog- and child-friendly gardens around a historic, oceanview home, and the luxurious, gourmet food-and-wine indulgence of the **Little River Inn** ($130 and up; 707/937-5942), where the same family has been welcoming travelers since 1939.

Anderson Valley

From Hwy-1 south of Mendocino, Hwy-128 cuts diagonally across to US-101 through the lovely **Anderson Valley,** home to numerous fine wineries (including Husch, Navarro, and Kendall-Jackson) and the *Anderson Valley Advertiser,* one of California's most outspoken local newspapers. Anderson Valley also has its own regional dialect, called "Boontling," combining English, Scots-Irish, Spanish, and Native American words into a lighthearted lingo created, some say, simply to befuddle outsiders—or "shark the bright-lighters," in the local lingo.

To find out more, stop in the valley's tiny main town, **Boonville,** at the All That Good Stuff gift shop and ad hoc information center. Fans of local food and wine will want to cross the highway to the **Boonville Hotel** ($185 and up; 14050 Hwy-128; 707/895-2210), a wonderful restaurant (dinner only, alas) and wine bar. The historic building has upstairs rooms filled with art and furniture made by local craftspeople. Beer fans can make a pilgrimage east of town (toward Ukiah) to the partially solar-powered home of the **Anderson Valley Brewing Company** (17700 Hwy-253; 707/895-BEER), where you can sample some of the world's best beers, including the legendary Boont Amber Ale.

Elk

While the coastal scenery is stupendous all the way along the Mendocino coast, one place worth keeping an eye out for on the drive along Hwy-1 is the tiny roadside community of **Elk** (pop. 250), 15 miles south of Mendocino. Elk is a wonderful little wide-spot-in-the-road, with what must be one of the oldest and most characterful service stations in California (the Elk Garage, in business since 1901) alongside a great little veggie-friendly breakfast-and-lunch road-food stop: **Queenie's Roadhouse Café** (707/877-3285). Elk also boasts a general store, some quirky cliffside cabins, and a steep trail leading down to the Pacific shore at Greenwood Cove. If you have the time and means for a splurge, the peaceful oceanfront **Elk Cove Inn** is a delightful small B&B inn ($100 and up; 707/877-3321).

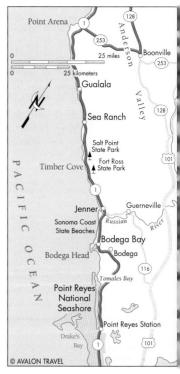

Point Arena and Gualala

With only a few exceptions, the southernmost 40 miles of Mendocino coastline are almost totally undeveloped and virtually uninhabited, with green forests and coastal coves as far as the eye can see. The westernmost point here, **Point Arena,** is about five miles northwest of Hwy-1 via Lighthouse Road (the namesake lighthouse, built in 1870, stands 115 feet tall). Back on Hwy-1, the small town of Point Arena is worth a wander for nice cafés and bakeries; try the fluffy quiches or buttery croissants at *le très* Francophile **Franny's Cup & Saucer** (213 Main St.; 707/882-2500), across the street from the lively Arena Theater, which puts on new-run movies nightly and good live music.

Another 15 miles south, situated at the very southern edge of Mendocino County, the old logging port of **Gualala** (pop. 585) has one truly remarkable feature: the Russian Orthodox domes of **St. Orres** (36601 S. Hwy-1; 707/884-3303), now a B&B inn and $100-a-head gourmet restaurant glowing with polished wood and stained glass, above Hwy-1 on the north side of town.

If you prefer to hang out with locals rather than well-heeled tourists from San Francisco, head instead to local bakeries like **Trinks Café** (707/884-1713) in the Seacliff Center shopping complex, or grab a BBQ brisket sandwich at **Bones Roadhouse** (707/884-1188), just north. Great camping and an incredible coastal panorama can be yours at **Gualala Point Regional Park** ($6 day, $30 camping; 707/785-2377), a mile south of town along the Gualala River.

Sea Ranch

Midway between Mendocino and the San Francisco Bay Area, the vacation-home community of **Sea Ranch** was laid out in the mid-1960s by an enthusiastic group of architects and planners including Lawrence Halprin and the late Charles Moore, who hoped to show that development need not destroy or negatively impact the natural beauty of the California coast. Strict design guidelines, preserving over half the 5,000 acres as open space and requiring the use of muted natural wood cladding and other barn-like features, made it an aesthetic success, which you can appreciate for yourself at the **Sea Ranch Lodge** ($179 and up; 707/785-2371), near the south end of the development.

The rest of Sea Ranch, however, is strictly private, which has raised the hackles of area activists, who after years of lawsuits finally forced through a few coastal access trails in the mid-1980s;

these, such as **Walk-On Beach** at milepost 56.5, are marked by turnouts along Hwy-1.

Salt Point State Park

The many sheltered rocky coves of **Salt Point State Park** make it ideal for undersea divers, who come to hunt the abundant abalone. Along these six miles of jagged shoreline, pines and redwoods clutch the water's edge, covering some 6,000 acres on both sides of Hwy-1 to make Salt Point a prime place for hiking and camping. For a guide to the 20 miles of trails, or background on the sandstone mortars and other remnants of the Kashaya Pomo tribal village that stood here until the 1850s, contact the visitors center (707/847-3221).

One of the few positive effects of cutting down the native redwood forests that once covered the Northern California coast has been the emergence of giant-sized rhododendrons in their place. You'll find the most impressive display at the **Kruse Rhododendron State Natural Preserve,** high above Hwy-1 adjacent to Salt Point State Park, where some 300 acres of rhododendrons, some reaching 14 feet in height, burst forth in late spring, usually peaking around the first week of May.

In between Salt Point and Fort Ross, Beniamino Bufano's 93-foot *Peace* statue looms like a shiny silver missile alongside Hwy-1 above craggy Timber Cove, where there's also a nice restaurant and inn ($140 and up; 707/847-3231).

Fort Ross State Historic Park

If you're captivated by California's lively history, one of the most evocative spots in the state is **Fort Ross State Historic Park,** the well-restored remains of a Russian fur-trapping outpost built here in 1812. During a 30-year residency, the Russians farmed wheat and potatoes, traded with native tribes, and trapped local seals and sea otters for their furs, which commanded huge sums on the European market. By 1840, the near-destruction of the sea otter population caused the company to shut down operations and sell the fort to Sacramento's John Sutter, who financed the purchase on credit. Later, the abandoned fort was badly damaged by the 1906 San Francisco earthquake and later fires, but the state has completed a high-quality restoration and reconstruction project, using hand-hewn

Bohemian Grove, the world's most exclusive men's club, covers 2,700 acres of redwood forest just south of the Russian River outside the village of Monte Rio.

Russian Orthodox chapel at Fort Ross

lumber and historically accurate building methods to replicate the original barracks and other buildings, including a luminous redwood chapel.

Fort Ross spreads west from Hwy-1, 20 miles south of Sea Ranch and a dozen miles north of the Russian River. Outside the fort's walls, a modern **visitors center** (daily; $8 per car; 707/847-3286) traces the site's natural, native, and Russian history, and offers information on the park's many fine hiking trails.

Jenner, Guerneville, and the Russian River

South of Fort Ross, Hwy-1 climbs high above the rugged coastline, offering breathtaking vistas of the Pacific Ocean hundreds of feet below. Twelve miles south of Fort Ross, Hwy-1 reaches the low-key resort community of **Jenner** (pop. 170), which stretches along the broad mouth of the Russian River. Harbor seals and sea lions sun themselves on the beach at Goat Rock, houses climb the steep hillsides, and there's also a gas station, a post office, and the excellent **River's End** (closed Tues. and Wed.; 707/865-2484), which has a range of great food (everything from burgers to Indonesian-spiced seafood) and oceanview tables (inside and outside, depending on the weather).

the closing of the Russian River ferry, c. 1931

From Jenner, Hwy-116 runs east along the river, passing through forests, vineyards, and popular summertime resort towns, the largest of which is **Guerneville,** 13 miles away, with a number of worthwhile cafés and a largely gay and lesbian summer population. A more traditional place, with a broad but gravelly beach, boat rentals, cabins, and riverfront camping, is **Johnson's Beach & Resort** (16241 1st St.; 707/869-2022). After 35-odd miles, Hwy-116 eventually links up with the US-101 freeway to and from San Francisco, providing a faster alternative to coastal Hwy-1.

Sonoma Coast State Park

South of Jenner and the Russian River, Hwy-1 hugs the coast along 10 miles of rocky coves and sandy beaches, collectively protected as **Sonoma Coast State Park** (707/875-3483). Starting with Goat Rock at the southern lip of the Russian River mouth, a bluff-top trail leads south past intriguingly named and usually unpopulated pocket strands like Blind Beach, Schoolhouse Beach, Shell Beach, Wright's Beach (site of the park's main beachfront campground), and Salmon Creek Beach.

While hiking along the Sonoma Coast, be careful: Many people have been drowned by "sleeper" waves, which rise unannounced and sweep people off the rocky shore.

At the southernmost end, Sonoma Coast State Park broadens to include the wildflower-covered granite promontory of **Bodega Head,** which juts into the Pacific and provides a great vantage point for watching the gray whale migrations in winter.

Bodega Bay

Protected by the massive bulk of Bodega Head, the fishing harbor of Bodega Bay has grown into an upscale vacation destination, with Sea Ranch–style vacation homes lining the fairways of golf resorts and deluxe hotels overlooking the still-busy commercial wharves. On the waterfront, the **Lucas Wharf Restaurant & Bar** (595 S. Hwy-1; 707/875-3522) dishes up fish-and-chips and clam chowder; nearby **The Tides Wharf Restaurant** (707/875-3652) is bigger and has a large fresh-fish market.

South of Bodega Bay, Hwy-1 cuts inland around the marshy coastal estuaries, passing by the photogenic small town of **Bodega,** whose church Alfred Hitchcock used for many of the scariest scenes in his 1963 movie, *The Birds.* A little later, and a lot more uplifting, in 1976 international artists Christo and

Jeanne-Claude used Bodega as a key tableau in their installation *Running Fence,* which draped an 18-foot-high, nearly 25-mile-long fabric curtain across the rolling ranchlands, from the coast to the inland valleys.

Valley Ford

Bodega's church, used by Alfred Hitchcock in *The Birds*

Between Bodega Bay and Point Reyes, Hwy-1 veers inland to avoid the marshy lowlands, and midway between the two bigger destinations the winding two-lane highway brings you to a great road trip stop. **Valley Ford** is a photogenic community that holds a great old family-run roadhouse, **Dinucci's** (707/876-3260), serving huge portions of unreconstructed Italian food—minestrone, fresh bread, salad, and pasta—for around $10 to $20 per person (dinner only, plus lunch on Sun.). More self-consciously stylish, contemporary fare is on the menu next door at quirky **Rocker Oysterfeller's** (dinner Wed.–Sun., lunch Sat., and brunch Sun.; 707/876-1983), inside the Civil War–era Valley Ford Hotel, which has been renovated with luxurious rooms while retaining old-time charm (quilts on the beds, rocking chairs on the porch, the whole nine yards).

Point Reyes

Between Bodega Bay and the Golden Gate Bridge, Hwy-1 slices through one of the country's most scenically and economically wealthy areas, **Marin County.** Though less than an hour from San Francisco, the northwestern reaches of the county are surprisingly rural, consisting of rolling dairylands and a few untouched small towns; Hwy-1 follows a slow and curving route along the usually uncrowded two-lane blacktop.

After looping inland south of Bodega Bay, Hwy-1 reaches the shore again at oyster-rich **Tomales Bay,** around which it winds for a dozen or so miles before reaching the earthy but erudite town of **Point Reyes Station.** Here the excellent **Station House Cafe** (closed Wed.; 11180 Hwy-1; 415/663-1515) serves incredibly good breakfasts and delicious lunches that include great-

A sign outside the small white garage on Main Street in Point Reyes Station claims it is the oldest Chevrolet dealer in California.

tasting local oysters, on the half-shell or barbecued. The bar is lively and well-stocked, and hosts free live music most Sunday afternoons.

Northwest from town along Sir Francis Drake Boulevard, the 70,000-plus-acre **Point Reyes National Seashore** offers an entire guidebook's worth of hiking and cycling trails, broad beaches, dense forests, and more; stop at the **Bear Valley Visitor Center** (daily; free; 415/464-5100) for more information. The photogenic lighthouse at the tip of Point Reyes gives great views over the coast, and in winter and spring (Dec.–June) the steep headland makes an ideal spot for watching migrating gray whales.

Eight miles from the visitors center, the **HI-Point Reyes Hostel** (1390 Limantour Spit Rd.; 415/663-8811) has dorm beds in an old farmhouse on the road to Drake's Bay.

Dozens of delightful inns and restaurants operate in and around Point Reyes, but because they're a mere 35 miles from San Francisco, they're often booked solid weeks in advance. Everything from treetop rooms to waterfront cabins can be found through **Inns of Marin** (415/663-2000).

Bolinas and Stinson Beach

Sitting at the southern end of the Point Reyes peninsula, **Bolinas** is a small town with a well-earned reputation for discouraging tourists; the signs leading you here from Hwy-1 are regularly torn down by locals bent on keeping the place—little more than a general store, a bakery, and a bar—for themselves. Bolinas also boasts one of the coast's best tidepool areas in **Duxbury Reef,** which curves around the western edge of Bolinas.

In contrast, the broad strands of **Stinson Beach,** four miles south along Hwy-1, are the Bay Area's most popular summertime sun-tanning spots. A grocery store and deli, the **Live Water Surf Shop** (which rents boards and the essential wetsuits), and a couple of outdoor bar-and-grills along Hwy-1 form a short parade at the entrance to the beach. The best place to eat hereabouts is the **Parkside Cafe** (43 Arenal Ave.; 415/868-1272); if you want to stay overnight, try the basic but cheap **Stinson Beach Motel** ($95 and up; 3416 Hwy-1; 415/868-1712).

If you have the chance to plan ahead, try to book a night at the **Steep Ravine Cabins** (800/444-7275), just over a mile south of Stinson Beach on the ocean side of Hwy-1. Now part of Mt. Tamalpais State Park, these 10 rustic redwood cabins are very basic roof-over-the-head accommodations (bring sleeping bags and food; water faucets are just outside the door) in an absolutely beautiful coastal chasm. These very popular cabins (originally owned by Bay Area bigwigs like Dorothea Lange) sleep up to five people and cost around $75 a night.

Mt. Tamalpais, Muir Woods, and Muir Beach

From the coast, a pair of roads—Panoramic Highway and the Shoreline Highway (Hwy-1)—twist up and over the slopes of **Mt. Tamalpais** (elev. 2,586), the signature peak of the San Francisco Bay Area. Known usually as "Mt. Tam," the whole mountain has been protected in semi-natural state within a series of state and national parks, and its voluptuous slopes offer incredible views of the urbanized Bay Area and the

untouched coastline; drive to within 100 yards of the top for a 360-degree panorama, or stop at the Pantoll **ranger station**

The all-terrain mountain bike, which now accounts for half of all bikes on (and off) the roads, was invented in the late 1970s by a group of daredevil Marin cyclists intent on cruising down the fire roads of Mt. Tamalpais at the highest possible speed.

(415/388-2070) for a map of Mt. Tam's hiking routes and fire roads.

If you plan ahead, you may also be able to spend the night on the mountain, indoors, in the comfort of **The West Point Inn** (around $50 per person; 415/646-0702), a hiker-centric, walk-in only lodge (two miles from Pantoll), that was built back in 1904 as part of a long-vanished scenic railroad, whose right-of-way is now one of Mt. Tam's most popular hiking trails.

A deep, dark valley between the coast and Mt. Tamalpais holds the last surviving stand of Marin County redwoods, preserved for future generations as the **Muir Woods National Monument** (daily 8 AM–dusk; $5) and named in honor of turn-of-the-20th-century naturalist John Muir. A paved, mile-long trail takes in the biggest trees, but since the park is often crowded with busloads of sightseeing hordes making the tour from San Francisco, you may want to explore the farther-flung areas, climbing up Mt.

view from atop Mt. Tamalpais

Tamalpais or following Muir Creek two miles downstream to the crescent-shaped cove of **Muir Beach,** along Hwy-1. Besides stunning scenery, Muir Beach is also home to the welcoming **Pelican Inn,** an "Olde English"–style pub serving food and fine beers; overnight guests get cozy rooms and access to a delightful room called "The Snug," with a fireplace (rooms $190 and up; 415/383-6000).

Another enjoyably ersatz experience awaits at the junction of Hwy-1 and the US-101 freeway, where a historic roadside restaurant has been resurrected as the **Buckeye Roadhouse,** near Mill Valley (15 Shoreline Hwy.; 415/331-2600), where you can feast on fine barbecue, great steaks and burgers, and delicious desserts in a lively, retro–Route 66 atmosphere.

Marin Headlands

If you can avoid the magnetic pull of the Golden Gate Bridge and San Francisco, take the very last turnoff from US-101 (northbound drivers take the second turnoff after crossing the bridge) and head west to the **Marin Headlands,** a former military base that's been turned back into coastal semi-wilderness. A tortuous road twists along the face of 300-foot cliffs, giving incredible views of the bridge and the city behind it. The road continues west and north to the **visitors center** (415/331-1540), housed in an old chapel, with a reconstructed Miwok shelter and details on hiking and biking routes. And if you're so inclined, on Wednesday–Friday afternoons and the first Saturday of each month you can tour the world's only restored Cold War–era Nike missile silo (free).

Every June since 1905, one of the country's wildest foot races, the **Dipsea,** has followed a rugged 7.4-mile route from the town of Mill Valley to Stinson Beach. For more information, call the Dipsea hotline at 415/331-3550.

Nearby, the barracks of old Fort Barry have been converted into the very peaceful **HI-Marin Headlands Hostel** (415/331-2777), which has dorm beds for around $25 per person as well as private rooms.

Across San Francisco

From the north, Hwy-1 enters **San Francisco** across the glorious **Golden Gate Bridge,** where parking areas at both ends let you ditch the car and walk across the elegant 1.7-mile-long span. South from the bridge, Hwy-1 follows 19th Avenue across Golden Gate Park, then runs due south through the outer reaches of San Francisco, finally reaching the coast again at the often-foggy town of Pacifica. The most scenic alternative is the **49-Mile Drive,** the best part of which heads west from the bridge through the **Presidio,** along Lincoln Boulevard and Camino del Mar, following the rugged coastline to **Lands End,** where you can hike around and explore the remains of Sutro Baths, eat a burger or grilled cheese at **Louis'** (415/387-6330), a historic diner with amazing views, or dine at the wonderful (and not all-that-expensive) **Cliff House** (415/386-3330).

From Lands End, this scenic route runs south along the oceanfront Great Highway, which eventually links back up with Hwy-1 near the small but enjoyable **San Francisco Zoo** (daily; $15; 415/753-7080).

the opening of the Golden Gate Bridge, 1937

San Francisco

San Francisco is easily the most enjoyable city in the United States. Its undulating topography turns every other corner into a scenic vista, while its many distinctive neighborhoods are perfect for aimless wandering. Museums document everything from Gold Rush history to cutting-edge modern art, while stellar restaurants offer the chance to sample gourmet food from around the world—all in an easily manageable, densely compact small city.

view from inside Fort Point, with the Golden Gate Bridge overhead

If there's one place in the city you should stop to get your bearings, it's **Fort Point,** a massive, photogenic Civil War fort standing along the bay, directly beneath the Golden Gate Bridge. You can wander at will through the honeycomb of corridors, staircases, and gun ports, watch the fearless surfers and windsurfers offshore, and take in a panoramic view of the City by the Bay. From here you can walk up to and across the Golden Gate Bridge, or head west to Land's End or back into town via a popular bayfront walking and cycling trail. Another great place to get a feel for San Francisco is **Golden Gate Park,** which stretches inland from the western edge of the city, including more than 1,000 acres of gardens, a boating lake, and two landmark museums, featuring the copper-clad art of the De Young Museum, and the natural history, aquarium, and planetarium of the grass-roofed Academy of Sciences.

If there's one other place that ought to be on your S.F. itinerary, it's **Alcatraz.** Aptly known as The Rock, this was America's most notorious prison from 1934 until 1963. Now preserved as a historical park, the island is worth a visit as much for the views of San Francisco as for its grim past.

the Conservatory of Flowers in Golden Gate Park

To reach Alcatraz, take one of the ferries that leave throughout the day from Pier 41 at the east end of Fisherman's Wharf.

The **San Francisco Giants** (tickets $40 and up; 877/4SF-GTIX) play at retro-modern AT&T Park, along the bay in downtown's South of Market district.

view of Alcatraz as seen on approach by boat

Practicalities

San Francisco is one of the few cities on the West Coast where you really don't need a car, since distances are short and public transportation is quite extensive; the grid street plan makes it easy to find your way around. San Francisco's Municipal Railway's ("Muni"; 415/673-6864) network of public transit buses, trams, and cable cars will take you all over the city.

The only problem for visitors in San Francisco is deciding where to eat—there are so many great places that choosing among them can be a painful process. For breakfast, **Sears Fine Foods** (415/986-1160) at 439 Powell Street on Union Square is a local institution, as is the upscale **Fog City Diner** (415/982-2000) at 1300 Battery Street, which serves gourmet comfort food (and the world's best french toast) in a stainless steel supper club. Two more S.F. culinary landmarks are the **Swan Oyster Depot** (weekdays till 6 PM only; 415/673-1101 or 415/673-2757), a half block north of the California Street cable car at 1517 Polk Street, a simple oyster bar serving the city's freshest shellfish and coldest Anchor Steam beer; and **Sam's Grill** (415/421-0594), downtown at 374 Bush Street, with incredible grilled meat and fish dishes, melt-in-your-mouth shoestring fries, and ancient-looking 1930s wooden booths that seem like set pieces from a Sam Spade mystery.

Given San Francisco's worldwide popularity, it's no surprise that room rates run pretty high—expect to pay around $200 a night (including taxes). If you're here for a honeymoon or other romantic reason, the nicest place in town is the swanky **Mandarin Oriental** ($350 and up; 415/276-9600) at 222 Sansome Street, which fills the top floors of a Financial District skyscraper and has 270-degree bay views (even from the bathtubs!). The best budget options are the two HI hostels, one on the bay at Fort Mason (415/771-7277), another downtown at 312 Mason Street (415/788-5604); both cost about $25 a night. In between there are some nice motels on the outskirts of downtown, like the nouveau retro **Hotel del Sol** ($129 and up; 415/921-5520), in the Marina District at 3100 Webster Street.

The San Francisco Convention and Visitors Bureau (415/974-6900) publishes a good free street map and offers extensive listings of attractions, accommodations, and restaurants.

Since driving and parking in San Francisco can be frustrating and expensive (Steve McQueen could never make *Bullitt* in today's traffic!), consider parking out here in the 'burbs and taking public transportation into the center of town. The N Judah Muni trolley line runs between downtown and the coast just south of Golden Gate Park, via the Sunset District neighborhood, where parking is comparatively plentiful.

Montara and Princeton

From the San Francisco city limits, Hwy-1 runs along the Pacific Ocean through the rural and almost totally undeveloped coastline of San Mateo County. The first eight miles or so are high-speed freeway, but after passing through the suburban communities of Daly City and Pacifica, the pace abruptly slows to a scenic cruise. **Pacifica,** which has a long pier, a popular surfing beach, a bowling alley, an oceanview Taco Bell, and a handy Holiday Inn Express motel, makes a good edge-of-town base for seeing the San Francisco area. South of Pacifica, two-lane Hwy-1 hugs the decomposing cliff tops of Devil's Slide, where the terrifying old highway is being converted into a cycling and hiking path following completion of a long-delayed new tunnel (decades in the making).

The first real place south of Pacifica is the ramshackle beach town of **Montara,** where the old but still functioning lighthouse has been partly converted into the **HI-Point Montara Lighthouse Hostel** (650/728-7177).

South of Montara, Hwy-1 bends inland around the rugged shores of the **Fitzgerald Marine Reserve** (650/728-3584), a wonderful (but very fragile) tidepool area filled with anemones and other delicate sea creatures. The tidepools are visible at low tide only; look, but don't touch! Hwy-1 continues south past the Pillar Point Harbor at Princeton-by-the-Sea, where you can enjoy a different sort of sealife appreciation: the fresh fish-and-chips (plus nice wines and cold beers) at **Barbara's Fish Trap** (cash only; 650/728-7049).

Half Moon Bay

The first sizable coastal town south of San Francisco, **Half Moon Bay** is 25 miles from the city but seems much more distant. A quiet farming community that's slowly but surely changing into a Silicon Valley exurb, Half Moon Bay (pop. 11,324) still has an all-American Main Street lined by hardware stores, cafés, bakeries, and the inevitable art galleries and B&Bs. The main event hereabouts is the annual **Art & Pumpkin Festival,** held mid-October, which celebrates the coming of Halloween with a competition to determine the world's largest pumpkin—winning gourds weigh more than 1,500 pounds!

Until the construction of the $500-a-night beachfront Ritz-Carlton golf resort, the coastline of Half Moon Bay was almost completely undeveloped, but it's still pretty nice and accessible, with a four-mile-long string of state park beaches at the foot of blufftop vegetable farms and horse ranches. The town also retains its rural feel, but thanks to the presence of so many Silicon Valley billionaires just over the hills, it has significantly better restaurants. The best fish tacos (and great fish-and-chips) can be had at the **Flying Fish Grill** (650/712-1125), off Hwy-92 at the north end of Main Street, while excellent and not outrageously expensive Italian specialties are on the menu at **Pasta Moon** (315 Main St.; 650/726-5125).

Looking for the world's biggest waves? Head down to **Maverick's**, an offshore reef area off Pillar Point, three miles north of Half Moon Bay. In winter, when conditions are right, mega-waves as high as 80 feet draw expert surfers from all over the world. For a report, and a safety advisory to warn off any wannabes, call **Mavericks Surf Shop** (650/560-8088); it's located at Pillar Point Harbor, as near as you can get to the offshore breaks.

Pescadero and Pigeon Point Lighthouse

The 50 miles of coastline between Half Moon Bay and Santa Cruz are one of the great surprises of the California coast: The virtually unspoiled miles offer rocky tidepools and driftwood-strewn beaches beneath sculpted bluffs topped by rolling green fields of brussels sprouts, artichokes, and U-pick berry patches. Access to the water is not always very easy, and while surfers seem to park along Hwy-1 and walk across the fields to wherever the waves are breaking, for visitors it's best to aim for one of the half dozen state parks, like San Gregorio, Pomponio, Bean Hollow, or Año Nuevo.

The biggest town hereabouts, **Pescadero** (pop. 643) is a mile or so inland from Hwy-1 and well worth the short detour for a chance to sample the fresh fish, great pies, and other home-cooked treats at **Duarte's Tavern** (202 Stage Rd.; 650/879-0464), open daily for breakfast, lunch, and dinner at the south end of the block-long downtown.

Less than 10 miles south of Pescadero, the photogenic beacon of **Pigeon Point Lighthouse** has appeared in innumerable

Pigeon Point Lighthouse

TV and print commercials; the graceful, 115-foot-tall brick tower is closed, but the grounds are open for tours (Fri.–Sun. 10 AM–4 PM; donation), and the adjacent lighthouse quarters function as the very popular **HI-Pigeon Point Lighthouse Hostel** (650/879-0633), which has dorms beds, family-friendly private rooms, and a hot tub perched above the crashing surf.

Año Nuevo State Reserve

West of Hwy-1, one of nature's more bizarre spectacles takes place annually at **Año Nuevo State Reserve** (8 AM–dusk daily; 650/879-0227), where each winter hundreds of humongous northern elephant seals come ashore to give birth and mate. The males reach up to 13 feet head-to-tail, weigh as much as 4,500 pounds, and have dangling proboscises that inspired their name.

These blubbery creatures were hunted almost to extinction for their oil-rich flesh. In 1910, fewer than 100 were left in the world; their resurgence to a current population of more than 100,000 has proved that protection does work.

Every December, after spending the summer at sea, hordes of male elephant seals arrive here at Año Nuevo, the seals' primary onshore rookery, ready to do battle with each other for the right to procreate. It's an in-

Midway between Año Nuevo State Reserve and Santa Cruz, the **Davenport Roadhouse at the Cash Store,** on the east side of Hwy-1 in the village of Davenport, serves hearty breakfasts, lunches, and dinners. Tiny Davenport is also the birthplace of the **Odwalla** fresh-fruit-juice company.

credible show, with the bulls bellowing, barking, and biting at each other to establish dominance; the "alpha male" mates with most of the females, and the rest must wait till next year. Pups conceived the previous year are born in January, and mating goes on through March. During the mating season, ranger-led **tours** ($7; 800/444-4445) are the only way to see the seals; these tours are very popular, so plan ahead and try to come midweek. The three-mile walk from the parking area to the shore is worth doing at any time of year, since it's a very pretty scene and some of the seals are resident year-round.

Two miles north of Davenport, **Swanton Berry Farm** (831/469-8804) is one of the last pick-your-own farms on the California coast. It also sells delicious organic fruit pies year-round.

The only accommodation option along this stretch of coast is three miles south of the lighthouse, or two miles north of the entrance to Año Nuevo, at **Costanoa** ($89 and up; 650/879-1100). A stylish retro-modern eco-minded resort, open since 1999 on the inland side of Hwy-1, Costanoa has everything from a luxurious lodge to tent cabins (complete with saunas!). There's also a café and an adjacent KOA campground (650/879-7302).

Big Basin Redwoods State Park

The oldest of California's state parks, **Big Basin Redwoods State Park** (831/338-8860) protects some 18,000 acres of giant coastal redwoods. Established in 1902, the park has many miles of hiking and cycling trails high up in the mountains. The heart of the park is most easily accessible from Santa Cruz via Hwy-236, but a popular trail winds up from the coast to the crest, starting from Hwy-1 at **Waddell Beach,** a popular haunt for kite-surfers and sailboarders, who sometimes do flips and loops in the wind-whipped waves.

Santa Cruz

The popular beach resort and college town of **Santa Cruz** (pop. 55,600) sits at the north end of Monterey Bay, a 90-minute drive from San Francisco, at the foot of a 3,000-foot-high ridge of mountains. It's best known for its Boardwalk amusement

Natural Bridges State Beach, four miles south of Santa Cruz via West Cliff Drive, has a natural wave-carved archway and, in winter, swarms of monarch butterflies.

Santa Cruz has just about fully recovered from the 1989 Loma Prieta earthquake, which had its epicenter in the hills east of the city.

park, which holds the oldest surviving wooden roller coaster on the West Coast, and for the large University of California campus in the redwoods above. The city was named by Spanish explorer Gaspar de Portolá and shares the name Santa Cruz ("holy cross" in Spanish) with the ill-fated mission settlement begun here in 1777. Modern Santa Cruz was all but leveled by an earthquake in 1989 but has since recovered its stature as one of the more diverting stops on the California coast.

The downtown area lies a mile inland, so from Hwy-1 follow the many signs pointing visitors toward the wharf and the beach, where plentiful parking is available. Walk, rent a bike, or drive along the coastal Cliff Drive to the world's first **Surfing Museum** (open in summer Wed.–Mon. 10 AM–5 PM, the rest of the year Thurs.–Mon. noon–4 PM; donations), which is packed with giant old redwood boards and newer high-tech cutters, as well as odds and ends tracing the development of West Coast surfing. Housed in an old lighthouse, it overlooks one of the state's prime surfing spots, Steamer Lane, named for the steamships that once brought day-tripping San Franciscans to the wharf.

A large part of the Santa Cruz economy still depends upon visitors, and there are plenty of cafés, restaurants, and accommodation options to choose from. Eating and drinking places congregate east of Hwy-1 along Front Street and Pacific Avenue in downtown Santa Cruz, which has a number of engaging, somewhat countercultural book and record shops along with cafés like **Zoccoli's** (1534 Pacific Ave.; 831/423-1711), which has great soups and sandwiches. The best burgers, veggie burgers, and fries are a

Surfboard designs have come a long way.

block west of Pacific at **Jack's Hamburgers** (202 Lincoln St.; 831/423-4421). More good veggie food can be had at the **Saturn Café** (145 Laurel St.; 831/429-8505), while the stylish **Soif** wine bar (105 Walnut Ave.; 831/423-2020) has fine wines and tasty tapas-like treats.

Motels line Hwy-1, and some nice-looking Victorian-era B&Bs stand atop Beach Hill, between the Boardwalk and downtown, where the **Seaway Inn** ($68 and up; 176 W. Cliff Dr.; 831/471-9004) is nice, clean, and reasonably priced. You can also avail yourself of the **HI-Santa Cruz Hostel** (321 Main St.; 831/423-8304) with dorm beds in an immaculate 1870s cottage for less than $30 per person. Among the many nice B&Bs is the rustic **The Babbling Brook Inn** ($157 and up; 1025 Laurel St.; 831/427-2437 or 800/866-1131).

Santa Cruz Beach Boardwalk

The bayfront **Santa Cruz Beach Boardwalk** should really be your main stop; besides the dozens of thrill rides and midway games, it boasts the art deco Cocoanut Grove ballroom and two rides that are such classics of the genre they've been listed as a National Historic Landmark. The biggest thrill is the **Giant Dipper** roller coaster, open since 1924, a senior citizen compared to modern rides but still one of the top coasters in the country—the clattering, half-mile-long tracks make it seem far faster than the 55 mph maximum it reaches. Near the roller coaster is the beautiful Charles Looff **carousel,** one of only six left in the country, with 73 hand-carved wooden horses doing the same circuit they've followed since 1911; grab for the brass rings while listening to music pumped out by the 342-pipe organ, imported from Germany and over 100 years old.

Santa Cruz Beach Boardwalk

Along with these and many other vintage arcade attractions, the amusement park also features a log flume ride, a sky ride, a two-story miniature-golf course installed inside the old bathhouse, plus a bowling alley and all the shooting galleries, laser tag, and virtual reality machines you could want. The Boardwalk, which has a concrete concourse but retains a great deal of charm and character, is open daily in summer and weekends only during the rest of the year. Admission is free and individual rides vary in cost, with the Giant Dipper costing $5 a trip and all-day, all-ride passes priced about $30. For more information, call 831/423-5590.

Mystery Spot

In the hills above Santa Cruz, two miles north of Hwy-1, the **Mystery Spot** (daily; $6 per person and $5 per car; 465 Mystery Spot Rd.; 831/423-8897) is one of those fortunate few tourist traps that actually get people to come back again. Like similar places along the Pacific coast, the Mystery Spot is a section of redwood forest where the usual laws of physics seem not to apply (trees grow in oddly contorted corkscrew shapes, and balls roll uphill). Among those who study vortexes and other odd geomantic places, the Mystery Spot is considered to be the real thing, but you don't have to take it seriously to enjoy yourself.

Watsonville, Castroville, and Moss Landing

Between Santa Cruz and Monterey, Hwy-1 loops inland through the farmlands fronting Monterey Bay. Part freeway, part winding two-lane road, Hwy-1 races through, and to be honest there's not a lot worth stopping for: The beaches can be dreary, and the two main towns, Watsonville and Castroville, are little more than service centers for the local fruit and vegetable packers, though Castroville does have one odd sight: the "World's Largest Artichoke," a concrete statue outside a very large fruit stand at the center of town.

Coastal farms along Monterey Bay grow about 75 percent of the nation's artichokes, which you can sample along with other produce at stands along Hwy-1.

Back on the coast, midway along Monterey Bay, the port community of **Moss Landing** is a busy commercial fishery, with lots of trawlers and packing plants—not to mention peli-

In 1947, then-unknown Marilyn Monroe reigned as Miss Artichoke during Castroville's Artichoke Festival, still celebrated each May.

cans aplenty. Moss Landing sits alongside Elkhorn Slough, the largest and most wildlife-rich wetlands area in Monterey Bay (a busy nursery for baby seals, baby otters, and baby leopard sharks), which you can see in greatest comfort via pontoon boat tour (831/633-5555). Moss Landing is also home to the research arm of the Monterey Bay Aquarium, a nice KOA campground, an obtrusively huge electricity generating plant, and **The Whole Enchilada** (831/633-3038), which has spicy seafood right on Hwy-1, near the power plant.

Much of the bayfront north of Monterey formerly belonged to the U.S. Marine Corps base at Fort Ord. Almost the entire parcel was turned over to the State of California to house the **California State University at Monterey Bay,** which opened its doors in 1994.

San Juan Bautista

Away from the coast, 15 miles inland from Monterey Bay via Hwy-129 or Hwy-156, stands one of California's most idyllic small towns, **San Juan Bautista** (pop. 1,862). It centers upon a grassy town square bordered by a well-preserved mission complex, complete with a large church and monastery, standing since 1812. Two other sides of the square are lined by hotels, stables, and houses dating from the 1840s through 1860s, preserved in their entirety within a state historic park (daily; 831/623-4881).

Completing the living history lesson, the east edge of the square is formed by one of the state's few preserved stretches of El Camino Real, the 200-year-old Spanish colonial trail that linked all the California missions with Mexico. Adding to the interest, the trail runs right along the rift zone of the San Andreas Fault, and a small seismograph registers tectonic activity. (Incidentally, San Juan Bautista was where the climactic final scenes of Hitchcock's *Vertigo* were filmed—though in the movie, they added a much more prominent bell tower with a seemingly endless staircase.)

The town's main street is a block from the mission and is lined by a handful of antiques shops, Mexican restaurants, and cafés like the **Mission Cafe** (300 3rd St. (831/623-2220).

Monterey

The historic capital of California under the Spanish and Mexican regimes, **Monterey** (pop. 27,810), along with its peninsular neighbors Carmel and Pacific Grove, is one of the most satisfying stops in California. Dozens of significant historical sites have been well preserved, most of them concentrated within a two-mile-long walk called the Path of History that loops through the compact downtown area. Park in the lots at the foot of Alvarado Street, Monterey's main drag, and start your tour at **Fisherman's Wharf,** where bellowing sea lions wallow in the water, begging for popcorn from tourists. Next stop should be the adjacent **Custom House,** the oldest governmental building in the state, recently restored as the **Monterey State Historic Park visitors center** (daily; 831/649-7118); here you can pick up maps or join walking tours of old-town Monterey.

The internationally famous **Monterey Jazz Festival** is held every September. For performers, dates, and other information, phone 925/275-9255.

From the Custom House, which is now surrounded by the Portola Hotel & Spa, you can follow the old railroad right-of-way west along the water to **Cannery Row,** where abandoned fish canneries have been gussied up into upscale bars and restaurants—most of them capitalizing on ersatz Steinbeckian themes. The one real attraction here is the excellent **Monterey Bay**

jellyfish at the Monterey Bay Aquarium

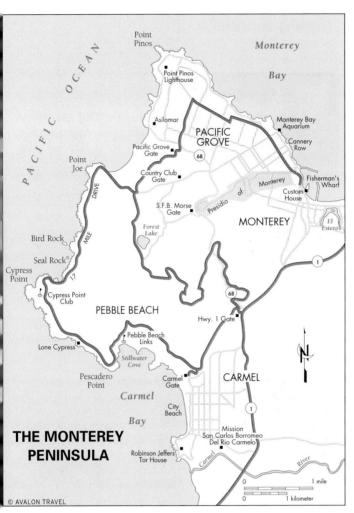

THE MONTEREY
PENINSULA

© AVALON TRAVEL

Aquarium (daily; $29.95; 886 Cannery Row 831/648-4800), housed in a spacious modern building and loaded with state-of-the-art tanks filled with over 500 species of local sealife. The aquarium is rated by many as the best in the world: Displays let visitors touch tidepool denizens, watch playful sea otters, gaze into the gently swaying stalks of a three-story-tall kelp forest, be hypnotized by brilliantly colored jellyfish, or face truly weird creatures that usually live thousands of feet below the surface of the bay.

Monterey Practicalities

Because Monterey gets such a considerable tourist trade, there's no shortage of restaurants, though good food at rea-

Hotel Del Monte, California, on Road of a Thousand Wonders

sonable prices can be hard to find. In the historic center of town, one good bet is the **Old Monterey Café** (489 Alvarado St.; 831/646-1021), serving large portions at breakfast and lunch. For breakfast near the aquarium, try **First Awakenings** (125 Oceanview Blvd.; 831/372-1125). For seafood, catch an early-bird special (before 6 PM) at one of the dozen restaurants on the wharf, or head a mile west along the frontage road to the very popular **Monterey's Fish House** (2114 Del Monte Ave.; 831/373-4647).

Along Hwy-1 on the northwest edge of Monterey, the elegant **Club Del Monte,** a grand resort that attracted the first wealthy tourists in the 1880s when it was called Hotel del Monte, is now part of the large U.S. Naval Postgraduate School.

Places to stay vary widely, starting with the **HI-Monterey Hostel** ($26 per person; 778 Hawthorne St.; 831/649-0375), in historic Carpenters Union Hall off Cannery Row, five blocks from the aquarium. Moderate motels line Munras Street along the old US-101 highway frontage south toward Carmel, while prices in downtown Monterey hover in the $200 range. One exception to the generally high prices is the refurbished and centrally located **Monterey Hotel** ($139 and up; 406 Alvarado St.; 831/375-3184 or 800/966-6490). Near the wharf is the beachfront **Monterey Bay Lodge** ($85 and up; 831/372-8057).

Many other nice places to stay and eat can be found in neighboring Pacific Grove or Carmel. For additional information on destinations from Monterey south to Big Sur, contact the Monterey County **visitors bureau** (831/649-1770 or 877/666-8373).

Pacific Grove

Perched at the tip of the Monterey Peninsula, **Pacific Grove** (pop. 15,041) is a quiet throwback to old-time tourism, dating from the 1870s when the area was used for summertime Methodist revival meetings. The revivalists' tents and camps later grew into the West Coast headquarters of the populist Chautauqua educational movement, based in upstate New York. The town still has a curiously Midwestern feel, from its many small churches to the rows of well-maintained Victorian cottages lining its quiet streets. Besides the many fine old buildings, the best reason to come here is the beautiful, fully accessible shoreline, which boasts some of the coast's best tidepools, sunset views, and endless opportunities for winter whale-watching.

Pacific Grove's main street, Lighthouse Avenue, runs through the 15-mph commercial district of cafés, galleries, movie theaters, and a small but excellent **Pacific Grove Museum of Natural History** (closed Mon.; free), which is a great option for kids or when the weather turns bad. Nearby **Peppers Mexicali Cafe** (170 Forest Ave.; 831/373-6892) serves very good, fresh Mexican food, while a range of fairly priced fish dishes are on the menu at **Fishwife** (1996 Sunset Dr.; 831/375-7107), near Asilomar, overlooking the wetsuited surfers riding the waves at Asilomar State Beach.

Places to stay in Pacific Grove are more reasonably priced than in Monterey or Carmel: **Andril Fireplace Cottages** ($140 and up; 569 Asilomar Ave.; 831/375-0994) is a lovingly maintained set of old-fashioned motor-court cabins, all with fireplaces and just two blocks from the ocean. The real landmark place to stay is the rustic **Asilomar Conference Grounds** ($95 and up; 800 Asilomar Ave.; 800/635-5310), on the coast, which has a lovely main lobby (with roar-

NATIONAL
**STEINBECK
CENTER**

The writer John Steinbeck lived in and around the Monterey Peninsula for many years and set many of his stories here, though things have changed so much in recent years that his beloved **Cannery Row** is hard to recognize. Steinbeck was born and is interred in **Salinas,** east of Monterey on US-101; after spurning him for most of his lifetime, the town in 1998 opened the **National Steinbeck Center** (1 Main St.) as a memorial to its literary son.

Pacific Grove is the best known of about 20 places in California where millions of migratory monarch butterflies spend the winter months. From October until March, the butterflies congregate on the Butterfly Trees, a grove of pines on Ridge Road off Lighthouse Avenue, well signed from downtown.

ing stone fireplace and heirloom pool tables) and some lovely, woodsy, Julia Morgan–designed cabins and lodge rooms, but is often filled with church groups or convention-goers. For a romantic getaway, it's hard to beat a Victorian-era B&B overlooking the Pacific from Lover's Point: **Seven Gables Inn** ($229 and up; 555 Ocean View Blvd.; 831/372-4341).

The 17-Mile Drive and Pebble Beach

Spanning the coast between Pacific Grove and Carmel, the **17-Mile Drive** is one of the most famous toll roads in the nation. Opened in the 1880s, the route initially took guests of Monterey's posh Hotel Del Monte on a scenic carriage ride along the coast through the newly planted Del Monte Forest between Carmel and Pacific Grove. Guided by Samuel F. B. Morse, son of the inventor, the formerly wild area underwent development beginning in the 1920s, first with golf courses like Pebble Beach and Cypress Point, and since then with resort hotels and posh homes.

Enter the drive at any of the gates, where you'll pay the toll ($9.50; bicyclists are free, and motorcyclists are banned) and be given a map and guide to the route, pointing out all the

scenic highlights, especially the trussed-up old **Lone Cypress,** legally trademarked subject of so many Carmel postcards. It's definitely worth doing the drive, if only to say you have, but to be honest, the views from the drive are no more or less splendid than they are from the toll-free drives, like Ocean View Boulevard in Pacific Grove, Scenic Road in Carmel, or Hwy-1 through Big Sur. You do, however, get to stop at the Lodge, where your toll will be deducted from the price of lunch or dinner. If you're in the mood to splurge on wanton luxury, you can also stay overnight at either of two extremely plush golf and tennis resorts: the modern, suburban-style country club of **The Inn at Spanish**

One event that brought Pebble Beach to national attention was the annual golf tournament hosted by Bing Crosby; originally an informal get-together, it grew into one of the main events of the professional circuit and is now the **AT&T Pebble Beach National Pro-Am,** held each winter.

Bay, which is also home to an Ansel Adams photography gallery, or stately, old-money **The Lodge at Pebble Beach.** Both resorts charge upwards of $600 a night; for details on accommodations (or Pebble Beach golf fees and tee times), call 800/654-9300.

Carmel

The exclusive enclave of **Carmel-by-the-Sea** (to give its complete name) began life in the early years of the 20th century as a small but lively bohemian colony inhabited by the literary likes of Sinclair Lewis, Mary Austin, and Upton Sinclair. However, with a few arts-and-craftsy exceptions, by the 1950s Carmel had turned into the archly conservative and contrivedly quaint community it is today—a place where Marie Antoinette would no doubt feel at home, dressing down as a peasant, albeit in Chaps by Ralph Lauren. Preserving its rural feel by banning street addresses (and home mail delivery), Carmel simultaneously loves and abhors the many thousands of tourists who descend on it every weekend to window-shop its many designer boutiques and galleries, which fill the few blocks off Ocean Avenue, the main drag through town. Though most of Carmel's many art galleries seem directed at interior decorators, a few are worth searching out, including the **Photography West Gallery** on the southeast corner

Every August for more than 60 years, Pebble Beach has drawn classic car collectors from around the world to show off their immaculately restored automobiles at the annual **Pebble Beach Concours d'Elegance.**

Carmel's leading light, Clint Eastwood, seems ever-present: Besides once serving as mayor, he owns the Mission Ranch resort. As a filmmaker, he used Carmel as the location for one of his most disturbing movies, the psychopathic 1970s *Play Misty for Me.*

of Dolores and Ocean, and the **Weston Gallery** on Sixth Avenue near Dolores Street, featuring the works of Edward Weston, Ansel Adams, and other Carmel-based photographers.

Though it's easy to be put off by the surface glitz, Carmel does have a lot going for it. The water is too cold and treacherous for swimming, but broad **Carmel City Beach** at the foot of Ocean Avenue gleams white against a truly azure cove. To the

Big Sur

Stretching 90 miles south of Carmel from Point Lobos all the way to Hearst Castle, Big Sur is one of the most memorable sections of coastline on the planet, with 5,000-foot-tall mountains rising up from the Pacific Ocean. Early Spanish missionaries dubbed it El País Grande del Sur (the Big Country of the South), and the rugged land has resisted development or even much of a population—the current total of around 1,000 is roughly the same as it was in 1900, and for the 3,000 years before that.

Hwy-1, the breathtaking drive through Big Sur, was finally cut across the very steep cliffs in 1937 after 20 years of labor and several fatalities. California's longest and most popular scenic route, it's an incredible trip. Like the Grand Canyon and other larger-than-life natural wonders, Big Sur boggles the mind and, in an odd way, can be hard to handle; you have to content yourself with staring in awestruck appreciation, taking pictures, or maybe toasting the natural handiwork with a cold beer or glass of wine at one of the few but unforgettable cafés and restaurants along the way.

However beautiful the drive along Hwy-1, it's also narrow, twisting, packed with sluggish RVers on holiday weekends, and every few years is closed by mud slides and washouts after torrential winter storms and the even more destructive wildfires that have plagued the coast in recent summers. In 1983, the biggest storm in recent memory closed the road for more than a year, and some scars from the 2008 fires can be seen inland from Big Sur Village.

Big Sur is still a very wild place (with little or no cell phone reception), and there are very few services, with most of the overnight accommodations booked up solidly during the peak summer season. Spring brings wildflowers, while fall gets the most reliably good weather. No matter when you come, even if you just drive through in an afternoon, be sure to stop whenever possible and get out of the car; scenic viewpoints line the roadside, and dozens of trails lead off into the wilds. The best basic guide to Big Sur is an annual free newspaper, *El Sur Grande*, published by Monterey County and available at ranger stations and many other locations in and around Big Sur.

south, aptly named **Scenic Road** winds along the rocky coast, past poet Robinson Jeffers's dramatic **Tor House** (tours Fri. and Sat. 10 AM–3 PM; $10; 831/624-1813). Jeffers, who lived at the house between 1919 and 1962, built much of what you see here out of boulders he hauled up by hand from the beach.

At the south end of the Carmel peninsula, another broad beach, **Carmel River State Beach,** spreads at the mouth of the Carmel River; this usually unpopulated spot is also a favorite spot for scuba divers exploring the deep undersea canyon.

Above the beach, just west of Hwy-1 a mile south of central Carmel, **Carmel Mission,** also known as San Carlos Borroméo de Carmelo (daily; $6.50 donation) was the most important of all the California missions, serving as home, headquarters, and final resting place of Father Junípero Serra, the Franciscan priest who established Carmel and many of the 20 other California missions, and who is entombed under the chapel floor. The gardens—where on weekends wedding parties alight from limos to take family photos—are beautiful, as is the facade with its photogenic bell tower. This is the mission to visit if you visit only one.

Carmel Practicalities

Dozens of good and usually expensive restaurants thrive in Carmel, but one place to see, even if you don't eat there, is the tiny, mock-Tudor **The Tuck Box** (daily; 831/624-6365), on Dolores Street near 7th Avenue. Dollhouse-cute, it serves up bacon-and-eggs breakfasts and dainty plates of shepherd's pie and meatloaf for lunch. If you'd rather join locals than mingle with your fellow tourists, head to **Katy's Place** (daily 7 AM–2 PM; 831/624-0199) on Mission Street between 5th and 6th, serving delicious waffles and some of the world's best eggs Benedict. For great, MSG-free Szechuan Chinese food at low prices (and minimal ambience), check out **Tommy's Wok,** on Mission between Ocean and 7th Avenue (831/624-8518); get your food to go, and wander down to the beach.

Carmel hotel rates average well over $250 a night, and there isn't any real budget option (apart from nearby Monterey). However, if you want to splurge on a bit of luxury, Carmel is a good place to do it. Besides the golf course resorts of nearby Pebble Beach, Carmel also has the commodious, 1920s-era, mission-style **Cypress Inn** at Lincoln and 7th ($225 and up; 831/624-3871), partly owned by dog-loving Doris Day (and featuring posters of her movies in the small bar off the lobby). A relaxing spot away from downtown is the historic,

Clint Eastwood–owned **Mission Ranch** ($120 and up; 26270 Dolores St.; 831/624-6436 or 800/538-8221), within walking distance of the beach and mission and offering full resort facilities and a very good restaurant.

Point Lobos State Natural Reserve

The sculpted headland south of Carmel Bay, now protected as **Point Lobos State Natural Reserve** (daily; $10 per car; 831/624-4909), holds one of the few remaining groves of native Monterey cypress, gnarled and bent by the often stormy coastal weather. The name comes from the barking sea lions *(lobos del mar)* found here by early Spanish explorers; hundreds of seabirds, sea lions, sea otters, and—in winter—gray whales are seen offshore or in the many picturesque, sea-carved coves.

The entrance to the reserve is along Hwy-1, three miles south of Carmel Mission, but in summer the park is so popular that visitors sometimes have to wait in line outside the gates. If possible, plan to come early or during the week. Whenever you can, come: Point Lobos has been lauded as the greatest meeting of land and sea in the world, and crowded or not it's definitely a place you'll want to see. Point Lobos has endless vistas up and down the rocky coast, and if you don't mind a short hike, there are a number of magical beaches hidden away at its southern end.

Garrapata State Park

The northern stretches of Big Sur are marked by the rugged coves, redwood forests, and sandy beach at Garrapata State Park, four miles south of Point Lobos. Though it's just minutes from Carmel, Garrapata could be light-years away from the crowds of shoppers and gallery-goers, but the two-mile-long beach here is pristine and easy to reach, yet generally empty. Winter wildlife-watchers sometimes see gray whales migrating close to shore, and if you really want to stretch your legs try the seven-mile Rocky Ridge Trail through Soberanes Canyon, which includes a steep descent (25 percent grade!) and heads east from Hwy-1 into a lush world of redwood groves, springtime wildflowers, seasonal streams and amazing views.

The highway clings to the coast for a dozen amazing but uneventful miles, passing a few languid cattle and an occasional vacation home before coming upon one of Big Sur's many unique sights, the massive volcanic hump of Point Sur, 19 miles south of Carmel. Though it's not exactly scenic or beautiful, it definitely helps you keep your bearings. A symmetrical, 361-foot dome, Point Sur is capped by a 120-year-old lighthouse, which has been preserved as a state historic park and is open for tours on Wednesdays, Saturdays and Sundays year-round, and Thursdays during July and August ($10; 831/625-4419).

Andrew Molera State Park

Spreading along the coast at the mouth of the Big Sur River, 20 miles south of Carmel, **Andrew Molera State Park** is a grassy former cattle ranch on the site of one of Big Sur's oldest homesteads. In the 1850s, immigrant Juan Bautista Roger Cooper bought the land and built a cabin in 1861, which still stands along Hwy-1 near the park entrance. Well-blazed but sometimes boggy trails wind along both banks of the river down to the small beach, horses are available for hire (831/625-5486), and there are quite a few nice places to camp (walk-in only). In winter, the park is also a popular resting spot for migrating monarch butterflies.

Big Sur Village

South of Andrew Molera, Hwy-1 cuts inland toward the heart of **Big Sur,** the deep and densely forested valley carved by the Big Sur River. Consisting of little more than three gas stations, a couple of roadside markets, and a number of lodges and restaurants, the mile-long village of Big Sur (pop. 950) represents the only real settlement between Carmel and Hearst Castle.

The photogenic **Bixby Creek Bridge,** 15 miles south of Carmel, was one of the largest concrete bridges in the world when it was built in 1932. The old coast road runs along the north bank of the creek, linking up again with Hwy-1 near Andrew Molera State Park.

At the north end of town, the **Big Sur River Inn** (831/667-2700) has a woodsy, warm, and unpretentious restaurant overlooking the river, and rooms upstairs and across the highway. Next door is a small complex that includes crafts galleries, a grocery store with burrito bar, and the homey **Big Sur Village Pub** (831/667-2355), which features good beers and pub grub. Continuing south, the next mile of Hwy-1 holds Big Sur's nicest group of rustic cabins and campgrounds: Besides a handful of quaint cabins in a quiet location, downhill from the highway and right on the riverbanks, **Ripplewood Resort** (831/667-2242) also has a friendly 1950s café on the east side of Hwy-1, serving very good breakfasts and lunches, as well as a handy gas station and general store.

At the south end of the Big Sur village, a classic 1950s motor court has been updated and restored to its original glory (now with free Wi-Fi!), as **Glen Oaks Big Sur** ($200 and up; 831/667-2105).

Pfeiffer Big Sur State Park

Roughly a half mile south of Big Sur village, **Pfeiffer Big Sur State Park** is the region's main event, a 1,000-acre riverside forest that's one of the most pleasant (and popular) parks in the state. Besides offering a full range of visitor services—restaurant, lodge, riverside campground, and grocery store—the park includes one of Big Sur's best short hikes, a three-mile loop on the Valley View trail that takes in stately redwoods, a 60-foot waterfall, and a grand vista down the Big Sur valley to the coast. The park also has the main **ranger station** (831/667-2315) for all the state parks in the Big Sur area. Just south of the park entrance, a USFS **ranger station** (831/667-2423) on the east side of Hwy-1 has information on hiking and camping opportunities in the mountains above Big Sur, including the isolated (but poison oak–ridden) **Ventana Wilderness.**

Pfeiffer Beach

South of Pfeiffer Big Sur State Park, halfway up a long, steep incline, a small road turns west and leads down through dark and heavily overgrown Sycamore Canyon, eventually winding up at Big Sur's best beach, **Pfeiffer Beach.** From the lot at the end of the road, a short trail runs through a grove of trees before opening onto the broad white sands, loomed over by a pair of hulking offshore rocks. The water's way too cold for swimming, but the half-mile strand is one of the few places in Big Sur where you can enjoy extended beachcombing strolls. The beach's northern half attracts a clothing-optional crew, even on cool, gray days.

Back along Hwy-1, just south of the turnoff for Sycamore

Canyon and Pfeiffer Beach, the excellent **Big Sur Bakery & Restaurant** (831/667-0520) makes its own fresh breads and pastries, brews a rich cup of coffee, and also serves full meals—soups, steaks, and wood-fired pizzas.

Ventana Inn & Spa and the Post Ranch Inn

South of Sycamore Canyon, roughly three miles from the heart of Big Sur village, Hwy-1 passes between two of California's most deluxe small resorts. The larger of the two, **Ventana Inn & Spa** ($400 and up; 831/667-2331 or 800/628-6500), covers 243 acres of Big Sur foothills and offers saunas, swimming pools, and four-star accommodations in 1970s-style cedar-paneled rooms and cabins. There's also a very fine restaurant, with incredible views and reasonable prices, to which guests are ferried in a fleet of electric carts.

Completed in 1992 and directly across Hwy-1 from Ventana, the **Post Ranch Inn** ($595 and up; 831/667-2200 or 888/524-4787), a low-impact but ultra-high-style luxury resort hanging high above the Big Sur coast, is at the forefront of luxury ecotourism. In order to preserve Big Sur's untarnished natural beauty, the Post Ranch Inn is designed to be virtually invisible from land or sea: The 39 guest rooms and two private houses—all featuring a king-size bed and a whirlpool bath with built-in massage table—blend in with the landscape, disguised either as playful tree houses raised up in the branches of the oaks and pines or as underground cabins carved into the cliff top. The Post Ranch restaurant, Sierra Mar, is also excellent, or if you want to have a look and plan for a future escape, free tours of the resort are given Monday–Friday at 2 PM.

The landmark red farmhouse along Hwy-1 at the entrance to Ventana was built in 1877 by pioneer rancher W. B. Post, whose descendants developed the Post Ranch Inn.

In 1987, the mighty California condor was all but extinct in the wild. Now, thanks to a successful captive breeding and reintroduction program, these massive birds can be seen soaring over the Ventana Wilderness that rises above Big Sur.

Nepenthe

One of the most popular and long-lived stopping points along the Big Sur coast, **Nepenthe** (831/667-2345) is a rustic bar and restaurant offering good food and great views from atop a rocky headland some thousand feet above the Pacific. Named for the mythical drug that causes one to forget all sorrows, Nepenthe looks like something out of a 1960s James Bond movie, built of huge boulders and walls of plate glass. The food is plenty good—burgers, steaks, and fish dominate the menu—but it's the view you come here for.

Sharing a parking lot, and taking advantage of similar views, the neighboring **Cafe Kevah** (831/667-2344) serves brunch all

day, plus good teas and coffees and microbrews on a rooftop deck; you'll find a gift shop downstairs selling top-quality arts and crafts and knitwear by Kaffe Fassett, whose family owns the place.

Right along Hwy-1, at a sharp bend in the road just south of Nepenthe, **The Henry Miller Memorial Library** (closed Tues.; 831/667-2574) carries an erratic but engaging collection of books by and about the author, who lived in Big Sur for many years in the 1950s.

Julia Pfeiffer Burns was a Big Sur pioneer whose family lived near Pfeiffer Beach and homesteaded much of this rugged, isolated area. In 1915, she married John Burns, a Scottish orphan who lived with the nearby Post family, and they continued to live and ranch at what is now Julia Pfeiffer Burns State Park until Julia's death in 1928.

A half mile south of Nepenthe on the east side of the highway, one of the oldest and most atmospheric places to stay is **Deetjen's Big Sur Inn** ($90 and up; 831/667-2377), a rambling and rustic redwood lodge built by a Norwegian immigrant in the 1930s and now a nonprofit, preservationist operation. Though the rooms are not available to families with young children unless you reserve both rooms of a two-room building, Deetjen's also serves Big Sur's best breakfasts and hearty dinners, at which all are welcome.

Julia Pfeiffer Burns State Park

If for some untenable reason you only have time to stop once along the Big Sur coast, **Julia Pfeiffer Burns State Park** (dawn–dusk daily) should be the place. Spreading along both sides of Hwy-1, about 14 miles south of Big Sur village, the park includes one truly beautiful sight: a slender waterfall that drops crisply down into a nearly circular turquoise-blue cove. This is the only major waterfall in California that plunges directly into the Pacific.

From the parking area, east of the highway, a short trail leads under the road to a fine view of the waterfall, while another leads to the remnants of a pioneer mill, complete with a preserved Pelton wheel. Other routes climb through redwood groves up to the chaparral-covered slopes of the Santa Lucia Mountains.

About six miles south of Nepenthe, or a mile north of the parking area at Julia Pfeiffer Burns State Park, a steep fire road drops down to **Partington Cove,** where ships used to moor in the protected anchorage. The last stretch of the route passes through a 60-foot-long tunnel hewn out of solid rock.

Esalen and Lucia

Three miles south of Julia Pfeiffer Burns State Park, the New Age **Esalen Institute** takes its name from the native Esselen Indian tribe who were wiped out by European colonizers. Founded in the early 1960s by free-thinking Stanford University graduates inspired by countercultural pioneers like Gregory Bateson and Alan Watts, and set on a breathtaking cliff-top site overlooking a 180-degree coastal panorama, Esalen offers a variety of religious, philosophical, and psychological workshops, but most visitors are drawn to its incredible set of natural hot springs, right above the ocean and open to the public 1–3 PM For information on overnight "personal retreats," or to make reservations for massages or the hot tubs, phone 888/837-2536.

The southern reaches of the Big Sur coast are drier and more rugged, offering bigger vistas but fewer stopping places than the northern half. The road winds along the cliffs, slowing down every 10 miles or so for each of three gas station/café/motel complexes, which pass for towns on the otherwise uninhabited coast. The northernmost of these, nine miles south of Esalen, and 25 miles south of Big Sur village, is **Lucia,** which has wonderful ocean views, a small restaurant, and 10 creaky cabins ($150 and up; 831/688-4884).

High on a hill just south of Lucia, marked by a slender black cross, is the Benedictine **New Camaldoli Hermitage,** open to interested outsiders as a silent retreat. For details, phone 831/667-2456.

Nacimiento-Fergusson Road and Mission San Antonio de Padua

Five miles south of Lucia, the narrow Nacimiento-Fergusson Road makes an unforgettable climb up from Hwy-1 over the coastal mountains. Though ravaged in places by wildfires, it's a beautiful drive, winding through hill-side chaparral and dense oak groves before ending up near King City in the Salinas Valley. One real highlight here is **Mission San Antonio de Padua** (daily 10 AM–4 PM; 831/385-4478), a well-preserved church and monastery that is still in use by a Catholic religious community. Because the road passes through sections of Fort Hunter Liggett Army Base, you may need to show valid car registration and proof of insurance. History note: All the land on which the Army base and mission stand belonged at one time to mining magnate George Hearst, whose land stretched from here all the way south and west to the coast at San Simeon, where his only child William Randolph Hearst later constructed Hearst Castle. Hearst's old hunting lodge has been restored and is now operated as an unusual B&B, called the Hacienda ($50 and up; 831/386-2262).

> The roadside along Hwy-1 in the southern half of Big Sur has been invaded by thick bunches of pampas grass that crowd out local flora.

Near the foot of the Nacimiento-Fergusson Road is one of the few oceanside campsites in Big Sur, and perhaps the most amazing place to wake up on the West Coast: **Kirk Creek Campground,** operated by the U.S. Forest Service (831/667-2423). The setting is unforgettable, but so are the dastardly raccoons who are fearless in their efforts to eat your lunch before you do.

Continuing south, Hwy-1 runs past **Pacific Valley,** then passes by a number of small but pretty beaches and coves before reaching **Gorda,** the southernmost stop on the Big Sur coast. Just north of Gorda, tucked away on a knoll just east of the highway, **Treebones Resort** ($169 and up; 877/424-4787) offers rustic yurts and a swimming pool.

San Simeon: Hearst Castle

At the south end of Big Sur, the mountains flatten out and turn inland, and the coastline becomes rolling, open-range ranch land. High on a hill above Hwy-1 stands the coast's one totally unique attraction, **Hearst Castle.** Located 65 miles south of Big Sur village and 43 miles northwest of San Luis Obispo, Hearst Castle is the sort of place that you really have to see to believe, though simple numbers—115 rooms, including 38 bedrooms in the main house alone—do give a sense of its scale.

Even if Hearst's taste in interior design (or his megalomania, which by all accounts was understated in his fictional portrayal in Orson Welles's *Citizen Kane*) doesn't appeal, Hearst Castle cries out to be seen. One of the last century's most powerful and influential Americans (the Rupert Murdoch of his day), Hearst inherited the land, and most of his fortune, from his mother, Phoebe Apperson Hearst (his father was George Hearst, a mining mogul), and began work on his castle following the death of his mother in 1919. With the help of the great California architect Julia Morgan, who designed the complex to look like a Mediterranean hill town with Hearst's house as the cathedral at its center, Hearst spent more than 25 years working on his "castle"—building, rebuilding, and filling room after room with furniture—all the while entertaining the great and powerful of the era, from Charlie Chaplin to Winston Churchill.

William Randolph Hearst

At Piedras Blancas, just north of Hearst Castle, the roadside along Hwy-1 has been taken over by herds of massive, bellowing elephant seals, a once-threatened but clearly resurgent species of massive pinnipeds who congregate here every winter to fight and procreate.

A small **museum** (daily; free) in the visitors center, next to where you board the trams that carry you up to the house, details Hearst's life and times. If you want to go on a **tour,** the Grand Rooms Tour (which costs $25) gives the best first-time overview, taking in a few rooms of the main house. There's also an Upstairs Suites Tour and a Cottages & Kitchen Tour; each costs $25 and takes around 50 minutes, not including transit time. All tours also come with the option of watching a 40-minute movie giving the background on Hearst and his house-building. Advance reservations (800/444-4445) are all but essential, especially in summer.

Since Hearst Castle is rather isolated, it's a good idea to stay the night before or after a visit at nearby San Simeon, which has grown into a massive strip of motels. There's a $45-and-up-a-night **Motel 6,** or opt for free Wi-Fi at the **San Simeon Lodge** ($49 and up; 9520 Castillo Dr.; 805/927-4601).

Cambria

Without Hearst Castle, **Cambria** would be just another farming town, but being next to one of the state's top tourist attractions has turned Cambria into quite a busy little hive. Apart from a few hokey, tourist-trapping souvenir shops at the north end of town, it's a casual, walkable, and franchise-free community of arts and crafts galleries, boutiques, and good restaurants; from Hwy-1, Main Street makes a three-mile loop around to the east, running through the heart of town.

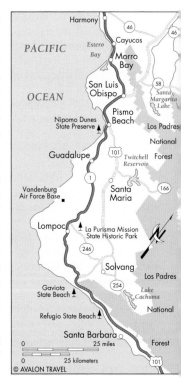

Above Cambria, a folk-art landmark known as **Nitt Witt Ridge** ($10; 881 Hillcrest Dr.; 805/927-2690) was built by the eccentric artist Art Beal, who used old Busch beer cans, seashells, roof tiles, and broken-down car parts to build, over 50 years starting in the late 1920s, what is often called a "Poor Man's Hearst Castle." The sprawling three-story house, with great views and intriguing details, is now open for tours.

Back in town, hearty breakfasts are available at the **Redwood Cafe** (2094 Main St.; 805/927-4830), while well-prepared multi-ethnic and vegetarian food is on the menu at **Robin's** (4095 Burton Dr.; 805/927-5007), a half block off Main Street. For barbecue, check out the cash-only **Main Street Grill** (603 Main St.; 805/927-3194). Places to stay range from nice older motels like the **Bluebird Inn** ($90 and up; 1880 Main St.; 800/552-5434) to the spacious suites and cabins at **Cambria Pines Lodge** ($109 and up; 2905 Burton Dr.; 805/927-4200), which has a nice pool high on a hill between town and the beach. For a relaxing overnight, try the lovely little **Bridge Street Inn,** a block from downtown (4314 Bridge St.; 805/927-7653), which offers very reasonable B&B rooms as well as shared HI-approved hostel beds.

Five miles south of Cambria, **Harmony** (pop. 18) is a former dairy town turned arts and crafts colony, with a range of galleries and a small wedding chapel.

Cayucos

Though it doesn't really look like much from Hwy-1, which has grown into a near-freeway to carry all the Hearst Castle traffic, the coastal town of **Cayucos** is definitely worth a look. Sitting along the coast 15 miles south of Cambria, not far from Morro Bay, Cayucos has a nice little beach, a fishing pier, a range of surfing and skateboard shops, and at least two unusual places to eat and drink. If you like tiki-style bars, you'll want to save your thirst for a visit to **Schooners Wharf** (171 N. Ocean Ave.; 805/995-3883), with good mojitos and variable food, served up in a landmark bar room downstairs, or on a oceanview terrace above. For good food, don't miss **Ruddell's Smokehouse,** just off the beach (101 D St.; 805/995-5028), where the no-frills menu features smoked salmon and tuna sandwiches, plus fish, pork, and chicken tacos.

Morro Bay

Marked by the Gibraltar-like monolith of Morro Rock, which was noted by Juan Rodriguez Cabrillo in 1542 and now serves as a peregrine falcon preserve and nesting site, **Morro Bay** (pop. 10,436) surrounds a busy com-

The **James Dean Memorial,** 27 miles east of Paso Robles near the junction of Highways 46 and 41, is a stark, stainless steel sculpture near the site where the talented and rebellious actor crashed in his silver Porsche and died on September 30, 1955. The highway has also been signed in Dean's memory.

Another San Luis landmark, the world's first motel, opened at 2223 Monterey Street in 1925. Originally called the Milestone Mo-Tel, the Spanish revival structure was later renamed the Motel Inn, but it went out of business long ago, and its remnants now stand next to US-101 on the grounds of the Apple Farm restaurant and motel.

mercial fishing harbor a half mile west of Hwy-1. A thin, three-mile-long strip of sand protects the bay from the Pacific Ocean, forming a seabird-rich lagoon that's included within **Morro Bay State Park,** a mile southeast of Morro Rock. There's an excellent museum ($3) with displays on local wildlife, and the park also contains the friendly **Bayside Cafe** (805/772-1465), serving lunch and dinner. Next door, when the weather's nice, you can rent **kayaks** 805/772-8796) and paddle around the estuary.

The rest of Morro Bay is pretty quiet; one unusual sight is a giant **outdoor chessboard** (with waist-high playing pieces) at the foot of Morro Bay Boulevard on the waterfront in City Park. For clam chowder or fish-and-chips, try **Giovanni's,** in the strollable waterfront neighborhood (1001 Front St.; 805/772-1276). Very good fast Mexican-themed "fusion" food is available at the **Taco Temple,** an often crowded and grandly named fish shack on the land side of the Hwy-1 frontage, a mile north of town (2680 Main St.; 805/772-4965).

San Luis Obispo

Located midway between San Francisco and Los Angeles at the junction of Hwy-1 and US-101, **San Luis Obispo** (pop. 44,174) makes a good stopping-off point, at least for lunch if not for a lengthier stay. Like most of the towns along this route, San Luis, as it's almost always called, revolves around an 18th-century mission, here named **Mission San Luis Obispo de Tolosa.** Standing at the heart of town, at Chorro and Monterey Streets, the mission overlooks one of the state's liveliest small-town downtown districts, with dozens of shops and restaurants backing onto Mission Plaza, a two-block park on the banks of Mission Creek.

Besides the mission and the lively downtown commercial

district that surrounds it, not to mention the nearly 20,000 students buzzing around the nearby campus of Cal Poly San Luis Obispo, San Luis holds a singular roadside attraction, the **Madonna Inn** ($179 and up; 805/543-3000 or 800/543-9666), which stands just west of US-101 at the foot of town. One of California's most noteworthy pop culture landmarks, the Madonna Inn is a remarkable example of what architecturally minded academic types like to call vernacular kitsch. Created by local contractor Alex Madonna, who died in 2004, the Madonna Inn offers 100 unique rooms, each decorated in a wild barrage of fantasy motifs: There's a bright pink honeymoon suite known as "Love Nest," the "Safari" room covered in fake zebra skins with a jungle-green carpet, and the cave-like "Caveman" Room. *Roadside America* rates it as "the best place to spend a vacation night in America," but even if you can't stay, at least stop for a look at the gift shop, which sells postcards of the different rooms. Guys should head down to the men's room, where the urinal trough is flushed by a waterfall.

Though the Madonna Inn has a huge, banquet-ready restaurant—done up in white lace and varying hues of pink—the best places to eat are downtown, near the mission. **Linnaea's Cafe** (1110 Garden St.; 805/541-5888), off Higuera, serves coffee and tea and sundry snack items all day and night; there's also the lively, veggie-friendly **Big Sky Cafe** (1121 Broad St.; 805/545-5401) and the usual range of beer-and-burger bars you'd expect from a college town. For something very special, the heart of SLO holds one of the central coast's great restaurants, **Novo,** serving locally sourced and very fresh Mediterranean-inspired meals on a nice terrace

A pedestrian walkway in downtown San Luis Obispo, off Higuera Street between Garden and Broad Streets, has become known around the world as **Bubble Gum Alley.** Since the 1950s, local kids have written their names and allegiances on the brick walls, using chewing gum rather than the more contemporary spray paint.

Every Thursday evening, the main drag of San Luis Obispo, **Higuera Street,** is closed to cars and converted into a very lively farmers market and block party, with stands selling fresh food and good live bands providing entertainment.

El Camino Real and the California Missions

While the American colonies were busy rebelling against the English Crown, a handful of Spaniards and Mexicans were establishing outposts and blazing an overland route up the California coast, along the New World's most distant frontier. Beginning in 1769 with the founding of a fortress and a Franciscan mission at San Diego, and culminating in 1823 with the founding of another outpost at what is now San Francisco, a series of small but self-reliant religious colonies was established, each a day's travel apart and linked by El Camino Real, The King's Highway, a route followed roughly by today's US-101.

Some of the most interesting missions are listed here, north to south, followed by the dates of their founding.

San Francisco Solano (1823). The only mission built under Mexican rule stands at the heart of Sonoma, a history-rich Wine Country town.

San Juan Bautista (1797). This lovely church forms the heart of an extensive historic park, in the town of the same name (see page 89).

San Carlos Borroméo de Carmelo (1771). Also known as **Carmel Mission,** this was the most important of the California missions (see page 97).

San Antonio de Padua (1771). This reconstructed church, still in use as a monastery, stands in an undeveloped valley inland from Big Sur in the middle of Fort Hunter Liggett Army training center. Monks still live, work, and pray here, making for a marvelously evocative visit (see page 104).

San Miguel Arcángel (1797). This is the only mission not to have undergone extensive renovations and restorations—almost everything, notably the vibrantly colorful interior murals, is as it was.

La Purisima Mission (1787). A quiet coastal valley is home to this church, which was restored in the 1930s using traditional methods as part of a New Deal employment and training project (see page 114).

Santa Barbara (1786). Called the Queen of the Missions, this lovely church stands in lush gardens above the upscale coastal city (see page 117).

San Gabriel Arcángel (1771). Once the most prosperous of the California missions, it now stands quietly and all but forgotten off a remnant of Route 66 east of Los Angeles.

San Juan Capistrano (1776). Known for the swallows that return here each year, this mission has lovely gardens (see page 132).

CALIFORNIA MISSIONS (1769 - 1823)

San Francisco Solano de Sonoma (1823)
San Rafael (1817)
San Francisco de Asis (1776)
Santa Clara (1777)
San Jose (1797)
Santa Cruz (1791)
San Juan Bautista (1797)
San Carlos Borromeo (1770)
Soledad (1791)
San Antonio de Padua (1771)
San Miguel Arcangel (1797)
San Luis Obispo de Tolosa (1772)
La Purisima Concepcíon (1787)
Santa Ynez (1804)
Santa Barbara (1782)
San Buenaventura (1782)
San Fernando Rey (1797)
San Gabriel Arcangel (1771)
San Juan Capistrano (1776)
San Luis Rey (1798)
San Diego (1769)

PACIFIC OCEAN

UNITED STATES
MEXICO

El Camino Real

0   50 miles
0   50 kilometers

© AVALON TRAVEL

backing onto Mission Plaza (726 Higuera St.; 805/543-3986). Great bar, too.

Along with the Madonna Inn, San Luis has a number of good places to stay, with reasonable rates that drop considerably after the summertime peak season. Besides the national chains, try the **Peach Tree Inn** ($79 and up; 2001 Monterey St.; 800/227-6396) or **La Cuesta Inn** ($89 and up; 2074 Monterey St.; 800/543-2777). There's also the **HI-Hostel Obispo** (1617 Santa Rosa St.; 805/544-4678), 28 beds in a converted Victorian cottage near downtown and the Amtrak station.

Pismo Beach

South of San Luis Obispo, Hwy-1 and US-101 run along the ocean past **Pismo Beach** (pop. 7,655), a family-oriented beach resort where the main attraction is driving or dune-buggying along the sands. Pismo was once famous for its clams, now over-harvested to the point of oblivion, but while you may still see people pitchforking a few small ones out of the surf, you won't find any on local menus. Like the rest of Southern California, the Pismo area has grown significantly in the past two decades, thanks mainly to an influx of retired people housed in red-roofed townhouses, but Price Street, the old main road running through the heart of the old small town, still offers a wide range of motels and restaurants, like the very popular **Cracked Crab** (751 Price St.; 805/773-2722), which has halibut and chips ($17) and a crazy range of fresh crab and other crustaceans (almost all of which come from Alaska). For a close approximation of Pismo's once-abundant clams, walk two blocks from the Cracked Crab, past the bowling alley, to another seafood specialist, the **Splash Café** (197

At the south end of Pismo Beach, beyond the scruffy farmlands that surround the wide mouth of the Santa Maria River, **Guadalupe-Nipomo Dunes National Wildlife Refuge** holds endless acres of windswept beaches, coastal sand dunes, and boggy bird-friendly marshlands, as well as the buried remains of a movie set used in Cecil B. DeMille's *The Ten Commandments*.

In 1936, Nipomo was the place where Dorothea Lange took that famous photograph of a migrant mother huddling with her children in a farm-worker camp.

Pomeroy Ave.; 805/773-4653), which is locally famous for its chowder served up in edible bowls made of freshly baked bread.

While Pismo is most popular for summer fun, every winter a grove of trees just south of downtown turns into a prime gathering spot for migrating monarch butterflies. The largest groupings, numbering in the tens of thousands though decreasing disturbingly quickly in recent years, are usually found roosting at the North Beach Campground of Pismo State Beach, along Hwy-1 off Dolliver Street.

Guadalupe and Santa Maria

South of Pismo Beach, California's coastal highways again diverge. Hwy-1 cuts off west through the still-agricultural areas around sleepy **Guadalupe** (pop. 6,296), where produce stands sell cabbages, broccoli, and leafy green vegetables fresh from the fields. The town itself feels miles away from modern California, with a four-block Main Street lined by Mexican cafés, bars, banks, and grocery stores.

If you opt to follow US-101, shopping malls and tract-house suburbs fill the inland valleys through rapidly suburbanizing **Santa Maria.** Among barbecue aficionados, Santa Maria is famous for its thick cuts of salsa-slathered barbecued beef, which can best be sampled at **Jocko's** (125 N. Thompson Ave.; 805/929-3565) in Nipomo, east of US-101 at the Tefft Street exit, where great steaks (and mouthwateringly moist, inch-thick barbecued pork chops!) highlight the no-frills menu. Barbecue is served from 4:30 PM daily.

Lompoc and La Purisima Mission

The rolling valleys around Lompoc are famed for their production of flower seeds, and consequently the fields along Hwy-1 are often ablaze in brilliant colors. Apart from colorful murals adorning downtown buildings, **Lompoc** as a town is not up to much, despite the unusual nature of the area's two main nonagricultural employers. One is a minimum-security federal prison; the other is Vandenberg Air Force Base, site of numerous missile tests, the aborted West Coast space shuttle port, and the $60 billion "Son of Star Wars" National Missile Defense program.

Lompoc flower fields

With its long arcade reaching across the floor of a shallow, grassy valley, **La Purisima Mission** (daily; $6 per car; 805/733-3713) gives a strong first impression of what the missions may have looked like in their prime. Four miles northeast of Lompoc, between Hwy-1 and US-101 on Hwy-246, the mission here was originally built in 1812 but fell to ruin before being totally reconstructed as part of a WPA make-work scheme in the New Deal 1930s. During the restoration, workers used period techniques wherever possible, hewing logs with hand tools and stomping mud and straw with their bare feet to mix it for adobe bricks. Workers also built most of the mission-style furniture that fills the chapel and the other rooms in the complex. Other features include a functioning aqueduct, many miles of hiking trails, and a small museum.

Buellton and Solvang

The town of **Buellton,** a block west of US-101 at the Solvang exit, holds one of California's classic roadside landmarks,

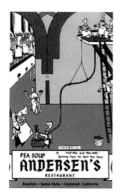

The late great pop singer Michael Jackson's **Neverland Ranch** lies here in the foothills of the Santa Ynez Valley, southeast of Solvang via the truly scenic Hwy-154, which loops inland south to Santa Barbara, arriving via a steep and stunning drive over San Marcos Pass.

Andersen's Pea Soup restaurant (805/688-5581), advertised up and down the coast. Another Buellton landmark, **The Hitching Post II** restaurant (805/688-0676), starred in the wine-loving road-trip movie *Sideways.*

Four miles east of Buellton and US-101, America's most famous mock-European tourist trap, the Danish-style town of **Solvang** (pop. 5,245), was founded in 1911. Set up by a group of Danish immigrants as a cooperative agricultural community, Solvang found its calling catering to passing travelers. The compact blocks of cobblestone streets and Old World architecture, highlighted by a few windmills and signs advertising the Hamlet Inn among many more suspicious claims to Danishness, now attract tourists by the busload. Many other U.S. towns (Leavenworth, Washington, and Helen, Georgia, to name two) have been inspired by Solvang's success, but to be honest there's nothing much to do here apart from walking, gawking, and shopping for pastries.

Just east of Solvang's windmills and gables, the brooding hulk of **Old Mission Santa Inés** stands as a sober reminder of the region's Spanish colonial past. Built in 1804, it was once among the more prosperous of the California missions but now is worth a visit mainly for the gift shop selling all manner of devotional ornaments.

Gaviota State Park and Refugio State Beach

Between Solvang and Santa Barbara, US-101 follows the coast past some of California's most beautiful beaches. Dropping through a steep-sided canyon, US-101 reaches the coast at **Gaviota State Park,** where a small fishing pier and campground are overwhelmed by the massive train trestle that runs overhead. Continuing south, US-101 runs atop coastal bluffs past prime surfing beaches, usually marked by a few VWs pulled out along the west side of the highway. Midway along this stretch of coast, some 22 miles north of Santa Barbara, **Refugio State Beach** has groves of palm trees backing a clear white strand. There's also a small, summer-only store, and a number of attractive campsites with hot showers.

Reservations for camping at Gaviota or Refugio, or at any California state beach, should be made in advance by calling 800/444-7275.

Rancho del Cielo, the ranch of former President Ronald Reagan, spreads along the crest of the coastal hills above Refugio State Beach.

Santa Barbara

The geographical midpoint of California may well be somewhere near San Francisco, but the Southern California of popular imagination—golden beaches washed by waves and peopled by blond-haired surfer gods—has its start, and perhaps best expression, in Santa Barbara. Around 100 miles north of Los Angeles, **Santa Barbara** (pop. 88,410) has grown threefold in the last 60 years, but for the moment, at least, it

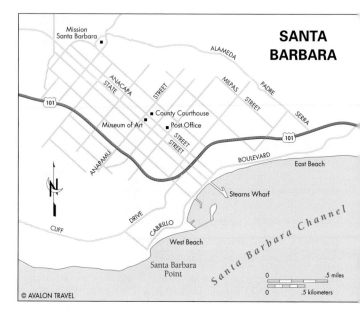

manages to retain its sleepy seaside charm. Much of its character comes from the fact that, following a sizable earthquake in 1925, the town fathers—caught up in the contemporary craze for anything Spanish Revival—required that all buildings in the downtown area exude a mission-era feel, mandating red-tile roofs, adobe-colored stucco, and rounded arcades wherever practicable. The resulting architectural consistency gives Santa Barbara an un-American charm; it looks more like a Mediterranean village than the modern city that, beneath the surface, it really is.

For a good first look at the city head down to the water, where **Stearns Wharf** sticks out into the bay, bordered by palm tree–lined beaches populated by joggers, in-line skaters, and volleyball players. From the wharf area, follow State Street away from the sands to the downtown district, where Santa Barbarans parade among the numerous cafés, bars, and boutiques. At the north end of downtown is the excellent **Santa Barbara Museum of Art** (closed Mon.; $9, free Sun.; 1130 State St.; 805/963-4364). A block east on Anacapa Street, the **County Courthouse** is one of the finest public buildings in the state, a handcrafted Spanish Revival monument set in lush semitropical gardens, with an observation tower (8 AM–5 PM weekdays, 10 AM–4:30 PM weekends; free) giving a fine view over the red-tiled cityscape.

Santa Barbara's reigning attraction, **Mission Santa Barbara** (daily; $5; 805/682-4713), stands atop a shallow hill a well-posted mile up from State Street, looking out over the city and shoreline below. Called the "Queen of the

Missions" by the local tourist scribes, Mission Santa Barbara is undeniably lovely to look at, its rose-hued stone facade perfectly complemented by the roses and bougainvillea that frame the well-maintained gardens and lawns.

Santa Barbara is one of many great places along the coast to go on a whale-watching cruise, on the *Condor Express* or other boats, to see migrating gray whales in winter and jumping humpbacks in summer. Trips take a half day or full day, and some head out to the Channel Islands; call 805/963-3564 or 888/779-4253 for details or reservations.

Santa Barbara has perhaps the coast's best variety of places to eat. State Street holds the most lunch and dinner places, like the old-fashioned burgers and beer on tap in the dark-wood dining room of **Joe's Cafe** (536 State St.; 805/966-4638). Great Italian food at fair prices has made a favorite of **Ca' Dario,** just off State (37 E. Victoria St.; 805/884-9419). There's excellent fresh sushi at **Arigato Sushi** (1225 State St.; 805/965-6074), while some of the world's best hole-in-the-wall Mexican food is served a half mile east of State Street at **La Super-Rica** (622 N. Milpas St.; 805/963-4940), where such distinguished foodies as Julia Child have come to chow down on a variety of freshly made soft tacos and delicious seafood tamales. It's not cheap, but the food is great (fresh tortillas, traditional *adobado*-marinated pork, and spicy chorizo), and the *horchata* is the creamiest you'll taste. Yum.

The city's accommodations, however, are among the central coast's most expensive, especially in summer when even the most basic motel can charge as much as $200 a night. One of the nicest of many motels is **The Franciscan Inn** ($114 and up; 109 Bath St.; 805/963-8845), just a short walk from the beach and wharf. At the top of the scale, the **Simpson House Inn** ($215 and up; 121 E. Arrellaga St.; 805/963-7067 or 800/676-1280) offers comfortable, centrally located B&B rooms. Off the scale completely, money's-no-object visitors can enjoy the deluxe facilities of the **San Ysidro Ranch** ($750 and up; 805/565-1700), in the hills above neighboring Montecito, where Jackie and JFK spent some of their honeymoon. Somewhat ironically, considering the generally high prices here, international budget chain Motel 6 got its start in Santa Barbara, where it now has five area properties, including the recently redesigned original one near the beach ($84 and up; 443 Corona Del Mar; 805/564-1392).

Channel Islands National Park

South of Santa Barbara, US-101 widens into an eight-lane freeway along the coast. Looking out across the Pacific, beyond the partially disguised offshore oil wells, you can't miss seeing

CAUSEWAY, COAST HIGHWAY, BETWEEN VENTURA AND SANTA BARBARA

the sharp outlines of the Channel Islands, whose rocky, tidepool-packed shores are protected as a national park. Consisting of eight islands altogether (five are part of the park), they sit from 12 to about 60 miles off the mainland. Numerous scenic cruises around the Channel Islands start from Santa Barbara, but only the closest, Anacapa Island, is easily accessible to the public, via daily trips from Ventura Harbor offered by **Island Packers** ($56; 805/642-1393). Bring water, as none is available on the island; camping is possible, but reservations are required.

Ventura

Midway between Malibu and Santa Barbara, downtown **Ventura** (pop. 106,433) is an offbeat little place, its three-block Main Street lined by enough thrift shops (seven at last count) to clothe a destitute retro-minded army. Apart from searching out vintage couture, the main reason to stop is the small and much-reconstructed **Mission San Buenaventura** (daily; $2; 211 E. Main St.), standing at the center of Ventura just north of the US-101 freeway. This was the ninth in the California mission chain, and the last one founded by Father Junípero Serra, in 1782. A block from

Ventura is the birthplace and headquarters of the outdoor equipment and clothing company Patagonia, started and still owned by legendary rock climber Yvon Chouinard.

the mission the **Albinger Archaeological Museum** (113 E. Main St.) collects a wide range of artifacts— the oldest from 1600 BC, the most recent from early American settlers—all excavated from a single city block–sized site alongside the mission.

Ventura doesn't get anything like the tourist trade that Santa Barbara draws, but it does have the very pleasant **Bella Maggiore Inn** ($75 and up; 67 S. California St.; 805/652-0277 or 800/523-8479), offering good-value B&B rooms in a nicely restored 1920s courtyard house between downtown and US-101.

South of Ventura, US-101 heads inland through the San Fernando Valley to Hollywood and downtown Los Angeles, while Hwy-1 heads south through the 10 miles of stop-and-go sprawl that make up the rapidly suburbanizing farming community of **Oxnard** (pop. 197,899), then continues right along the coast through Malibu and West Los Angeles.

Simi Valley

If you opt to follow US-101 rather than coastal Hwy-1 into Los Angeles, be sure to check out the somnolent suburb of **Simi Valley,** 30 miles east of Ventura, where the hilltop **Ronald Reagan Presidential Library** (daily; $12; 805/522-2977) fills 150,000 square feet of Spanish-style stucco with a fascinating array of exhibits and artifacts, most famously a chunk of the Berlin Wall, set in a Cold War–era tableau. Also here, housed in a 200-foot-long glass-walled pavilion, is the actual Boeing 707 used as presidential Air Force One by Nixon, Carter, Ford, Reagan, George H. W. Bush, Clinton, and George W. Bush. The "Great Communicator" was interred here following his death in 2004; to get to the library, take US-101 to Hwy-23 North (a.k.a. the Ronald Reagan Freeway), exit at Olsen Road, and follow the signs.

The other Simi Valley sight to see is **Bottle Village** (donations; 4595 Cochran St.; 805/583-1627), a complex of small buildings and sculptures built out of glass bottles, TV sets, hubcaps, and assorted other recycled refuse starting in 1956 by the late Tressa Prisbey. Subject of an ongoing battle between folk-art preservationists and those who think it's a pile of junk, the "village" can be viewed less than a mile south of the Hwy-118/210 freeway between the Tapo Street and Stearns Street exits.

Tressa Prisbey's Bottle Village

Pacific Coast Highway Beaches

Running right along the beach, the Pacific Coast Highway (Hwy-1) heads south from Oxnard around the rocky headland of **Point Mugu** (pronounced "ma-GOO"), where the U.S. Navy operates a missile testing center and the Santa Monica Mountains rise steeply out of the Pacific Ocean. Most of these chaparral-covered granite mountains have been protected as parkland, with hiking, cycling, and riding trails offering grand views and a surprising amount of solitude. Before or after a hike in the hills (or a Harley ride along the coast, the preferred mode of arrival), the ramshackle **Neptune's Net** restaurant (42505 Pacific Coast Hwy.; 310/457-3095) is a great place to hang out and "star"-gaze while enjoying fresh seafood, served up on paper plates for that down-home Hollywood feel.

South from here, state-owned beaches mark your progress along the coastal road, but this stretch is basically natural wilderness—apart from the highway, of course. Biggest and best of the beaches hereabouts is the lovely **Leo Carrillo State Park** (818/880-0363), which has a sandy strand, some great tidepools, and a sycamore-shaded campground (reservations 800/444-7275). Leo Carrillo (1880–1961) was an actor (he played Pancho in *The Cisco Kid* TV show) and preservationist who was instrumental in expanding the California state parks.

South of Leo Carrillo, which marks the Los Angeles County line, there are many more public beach areas, including (in roughly north-to-south order) **Nicholas Canyon County Beach, El Pescador State Beach,** and **El Matador State Beach** (where episodes of TV's *Baywatch* have been filmed). At big, brash **Zuma Beach County Park,** where volleyball courts and snack bars line the sands, the PCH highway bends inland around the headlands of **Point Dume State Beach,** a great spot for winter whale-watching.

Malibu

South of Zuma Beach, houses begin popping up along Hwy-1 to block the oceanfront views, and more-elaborate multimillion-dollar homes dot the canyons above as well, forming the sprawling exurbia and movie-star playground of **Malibu,** which stretches along

The main route inland from the coast, Malibu Canyon Road, was the setting of the key murder scene in James M. Cain's thriller *The Postman Always Rings Twice.*

Hwy-1 for the next 27 miles into Santa Monica and metropolitan Los Angeles. Unless TV helicopters are flying overhead to document the latest wildfire or other natural disaster, it's hard to get more than a glimpse of the garage doors or wrought-iron gates of these palaces, but this is the address of choice for the movers and shakers of the entertainment world: If you can name them, they probably own property here. Most of the truly huge estates are hidden away on ranches high up in the mountains.

One of these hideaways has been evolving since 1993, when Barbra Streisand donated her 22.5-acre ranch for use as a botanical preserve. Called **Ramirez Canyon Park** (5750 Ramirez Canyon Rd.), it's managed by the Santa Monica Mountains Conservancy and is open by appointment only, thanks to requests from neighbors.

From Hwy-1, the most prominent sight is the **Pepperdine University** campus, which was described by the late, great architect Charles Moore as "an overscaled motel set in obscenely vivid emerald lawns." Below the bluff-top campus, the legendary **Malibu Colony** of celebrity homes stretches along the coast in high-security splendor. Just north of Pepperdine, a short drive up Corral Canyon Road gives access to Solstice Canyon, part of the **Santa Monica Mountains**

Malibu Pier at sunset

Recreation Area, where a well-marked, mile-long hiking trail leads through scrubby native chaparral up to a delicate spring waterfall, past numerous signs of the frequent fall wildfires (like the 4,900-acre Corral Fire of November 2007, which destroyed Malibu's oldest home; the remains are preserved in situ).

Away from the mountains, about the only place in Malibu proper where it's fun (and legal) to explore is the area around the landmark **Malibu Pier,** which juts into the ocean at the heart of Malibu's short and rather scruffy commercial strip. North of the pier, which was used most famously in TV's *The Rockford Files,* stretches **Surfrider Beach,** site of most of those Frankie Avalon and Annette Funicello *Beach Blanket Bingo*–type movies made during the 1950s. The pier and the beach are part of **Malibu Lagoon State Park,** which also protects the historic **Adamson House** (Wed.–Sat. 11 AM–3 PM; $7; 23200 Pacific Coast Hwy.; 310/456-8432), a lovely old circa-1930 Spanish Revival courtyard home, right on the beach and full of gorgeous tile work and other architectural features. Tours of the house are given throughout the day, and fascinating exhibits portray Malibu history and the Rindge family, who once owned the entire region.

Just west of the pier and the Adamson House, another great place to get a feel for Malibu is at **Malibu Seafood** (25653 Pacific Coast Hwy.; 310/456-3430), a low-key beach shack drawing local gardeners, pool guys, and Hollywood starlets for BYOB fish-and-chips.

Topanga and the Getty Villa

Between Malibu and Santa Monica, **Topanga Canyon** is one of the last great wild spaces in Los Angeles, with a number of parks, trails, and perhaps the last wild and free waterways—steelhead trout still spawn in the waters of Topanga Creek, which flows down from the mountains to the Santa Monica Bay. Home to an alternative-minded community of some 8,000 hippies and New Agers (Neil Young recorded *After the Gold Rush* in his home here), Topanga was first established as an artists' colony in the 1950s by the likes of Woody Guthrie and actor Will Geer, who played Grandpa in TV's *The Waltons,* long after he'd been blacklisted during the anti-Communist McCarthy witch-hunts. For the past 30 years Geer's old property has been preserved as the **Theatricum Botanicum,** a garden and politically minded 300-seat open-air theater, six miles up the canyon (1419 N. Topanga Canyon Blvd.; 310/455-2322).

South of Topanga, and once again open to the public after a nearly 10-year, $275-million remodeling, are the world-famous antiquities of **The J. Paul Getty Museum.** Over 1,200 price-less classics are displayed in the pseudo-Pompeiian Getty Villa, where the oil magnate's art collection was housed prior to the construction of the massive Getty Center complex above Brentwood. Admission to the Getty Villa is free, but parking reservations ($15 per car; 310/440-7300) are essential.

From the Getty Villa south to Santa Monica, the Pacific Coast Highway (Hwy-1) runs along the wide-open sands of **Will Rogers State Beach,** gifted to the public by the Depression-era humorist.

Crossing Los Angeles

From Malibu and Topanga Canyon, Hwy-1 swoops along the shore, running along the beach as far as the landmark Santa Monica Pier before bending inland through a tunnel and meta-morphosing quite unexpectedly into the I-10 Santa Monica Freeway. The second exit off this freeway (which has been of-ficially dubbed the Christopher Columbus Transcontinental Highway, running all the way east to Jacksonville, Florida) takes you to Lincoln Boulevard, which carries the Hwy-1 moniker south through Venice and Marina del Rey to Los Angeles International Airport (LAX), where it runs into Sepulveda Boulevard.

After passing through a tunnel under the airport runways—worth the drive just for the experience of seeing 747s taxiing over your head—Sepulveda emerges in the Tarantino-esque communities of L.A.'s "South Bay," which utterly lack the glamour of chichi Santa Monica and Malibu. At Hermosa Beach, one of a trio of pleasant if surprisingly

Since Hwy-1 follows slow-moving Lincoln Boulevard and other surface streets across L.A., if you are in any sort of hurry you should stay on the Santa Monica Freeway (I-10) east to the San Diego Freeway (I-405), and follow that south as far as you're going. Coming from the south, follow these freeways in reverse order—or risk the time-consuming consequences.

Los Angeles

Love it or hate it, one thing you can't do about L.A. is ignore it. Thanks to Hollywood in all its many guises (movies, television, the music industry), the city is always in the headlines. Without falling too deeply under the spell of its hyperbole-fueled image-making machinery, it's safe to say that L.A. definitely has something for everyone. In keeping with its car-centered culture, however, our suggested tour ignores the many individual attractions and focuses instead on a pair of quint-essential L.A. drives.

the Los Angeles skyline, as seen from Mulholland Drive

Winding along the crest of the Hollywood Hills, **Mulholland Drive** is the classic L.A. cruise. Starting in the east within sight of the Hollywood sign and the Hollywood Bowl, this ribbon of two-lane blacktop passes by the city's most valuable real estate, giving great views on both sides, both by day and after dark.

Another classic L.A. cruise, running from the scruffy fringes of down-town all the way west to the coast, **Sunset Boulevard** gives glimpses into almost every conceivable aspect of Los Angeles life. Starting downtown, the historic core of colonial Los Angeles and now a showcase of contem-porary architecture thanks to a stunning new cathedral and concert hall, Sunset Boulevard's 27-mile course then winds west past Echo Park and Hollywood to West Hollywood, where it becomes the Sunset Strip, still the liveliest nightclub district in town. Continuing west, Sunset winds through Beverly Hills, Brentwood, and Bel-Air, lined by the largest mansions you're likely to see, before ending up at the edge of the Pacific Ocean.

The **Los Angeles Dodgers** (866/363-4377) play at beautiful Dodger Stadium, on a hill above downtown.

Practicalities

Most flights into Los Angeles arrive at Los Angeles International Airport (LAX), on the coast southwest of downtown, where you'll find all the usual shuttles and rental car agencies. Other useful L.A.-area airports include Bob Hope (BUR) in Burbank and John Wayne (SNA) in Orange County.

Gay and Happy Reveal Crowds Bathing in the Pacific, Santa Monica

Before choosing a place to stay, think about where you want to spend your time and settle near there. High-end places abound, but character can be hard to come by. Along the coast, recommended accommodations range from the handy **Santa Monica HI Hostel** (starts at $27 per person; 1436 2nd St.; 310/393-9913), a block from the beach, to the unique **The Queen Mary** in Long Beach ($104 and up; 877/342-0738), a hotel offering authentic art deco–era staterooms in the fabulous old luxury liner. Midrange with a great mid-city location, try the **Farmer's Daughter Hotel** ($189 and up; 115 S. Fairfax Ave.; 323/937-3930), next to the historic Farmers Market, a very friendly 1950s-style motel with tons of charm and the city's hottest new shopping mall and entertainment complex, The Grove, across the street. Downtown, the most fabulous place to stay is the retro-1960s **The Standard**

The Queen Mary

Downtown LA, ($155 and up; 550 S. Flower St.; 213/892-8080), with the world's coolest rooftop, poolside bar.

For food, one place I always try to stop is **The Apple Pan** (10801 W. Pico Blvd.; 310/475-3585), an ancient (circa-1947) landmark on the West L.A. landscape, serving the best hamburgers on the planet—though I'll admit to being biased, since I grew up eating them. Take a seat at the counter, and be sure to save room for a slice of the wonderful fruit pies. Late at night, the huge sandwiches and heart-warming soups at **Canter's Deli** (open daily 24 hours; 419 N. Fairfax Ave.; 323/651-2030) draw all kinds of night owls to a lively New York–style deli in the heart of the predominantly Jewish Fairfax District. Downtown, in the heart of old L.A., **Philippe The Original** (1001 N. Alameda St.; 213/628-3781), famous for its French dip sandwiches, is a classic workers' cafeteria, offering good food at impossibly low prices, with character to spare.

The usual array of information about hotels, restaurants, tickets to TV show tapings, and all other L.A.-area attractions is available through the **Los Angeles Convention and Visitors Bureau** (213/689-8822 or 800/228-2452), with an office at 685 South Figueroa Street.

blue-collar beach towns, Sepulveda Boulevard changes its name to Pacific Coast Highway, then bends inland to bypass the ritzy communities of the Palos Verdes Peninsula, passing instead through the industrial precincts of San Pedro that border the Los Angeles/Long Beach harbor, one of the busiest on the West Coast.

Long Beach

Directly south of downtown Los Angeles, the city of **Long Beach** (pop. 462,257) is the second-largest of L.A.'s constituent cities, but it feels more like the Midwest than the cutting-edge West Coast. Long Beach is probably best known as the home of the cruise ship RMS *Queen Mary,* one of the largest and most luxurious liners ever to set sail. Impossible to miss as it looms over Long Beach harbor, the stately ship is open for self-guided tours ($25; 877/342-0738). You can also stay overnight in one of the many staterooms and cabins, traveling back to a more elegant time for surprisingly reasonable overnight rates.

In place of Howard Hughes's famous "Spruce Goose" airplane, which used to stand next door, there's now a Cold War–era submarine, and across the bay on the main downtown Long Beach waterfront, the **Aquarium of the Pacific** (daily; $24.95; 562/590-3100) explores the diverse ecosystems of the Pacific Ocean, from tropical coral reefs (shown off in an amazing, 350,000-gallon display) to the frigid waters of the Bering Sea. The tanks full of jellyfish of all kinds, colors, and sizes are the main event.

Other Long Beach attractions include the "World's Largest Mural," a 115,000-square-foot painting of migrating gray whales on the outside of the Long Beach Arena, and the self-proclaimed "Skinniest House in the USA" (708 Gladys Ave.).

Long Beach also marks the southern end of L.A.'s reborn streetcar and subway system, and you can ride the Blue Line north to downtown and connect to everywhere else. It's an inexpensive base for exploring the Los Angeles area, especially if you avail yourself of the **HI-South Bay Hostel** (3601 S. Gaffey St.; 310/831-8109), in a peaceful locale on a hill overlooking the harbor area. There's also a **Best Western** ($100 and up; 1725 Long Beach Blvd.; 562/599-5555) directly across from a Blue Line train stop.

Huntington Beach

Winding south and east from Long Beach, Hwy-1 continues along the coast past a series of natural marshlands and small-craft marinas. The first real point of interest is the town of **Huntington Beach** (pop. 189,992), one of the largest communities in Orange County. Incorporated in 1909 and developed by Henry Huntington as a stop along his legendary Pacific Electric "Red Car" interurban railway network, Huntington Beach is best known as one of the places where **surfing** really took off on the U.S. mainland. To attract Angelenos down to his new town, Huntington hired Hawaiians to demonstrate the sport, which at the time made use of huge solid wooden boards, 15 feet long and weighing around 150 pounds. Huntington Beach, especially around the pier, is still a very popular surfing spot—though contemporary surfers slice through the waves on high-tech foam-core boards, a third the size of the original Hawaiian long boards. The history and culture of West Coast surfing, with examples of boards then and now (plus special collections highlighting surf movies and the creation of surf music by local heroes Leo Fender and Dick Dale), is recounted in the fantastic **International Surfing Museum** (daily; hours vary; donations; 411 Olive Ave.; 714/960-3483), two blocks from the pier in the heart of the lively downtown business district.

Anaheim: Disneyland Resort

Like a little bit of middle America grafted onto the southern edge of Los Angeles, inland Orange County used to feel like a totally different world. Though the area's demographics have changed considerably in the past decade or two, becoming more a part of L.A.'s fast-paced, edgily creative multiethnic stew, Orange County in the 1950s and 1960s was suburban America writ large—mostly white, mostly well-off, and absolutely, totally bland. In short, a perfect place to build the ultimate escapist fantasy, the self-proclaimed "Happiest Place on Earth," **Disneyland.**

inside "it's a small world" at Disneyland

The phenomenon of Disneyland has been done to death by all sorts of social critics, but the truth is, it can be great fun—provided you visit out of season, get there early to avoid the crowds, and really immerse yourself in the extroverted, mindless joy of it all. (Being here in the company of appreciative 8- to 12-year-olds is probably the best way to maximize your enjoyment.)

If you haven't been before, or not for a while at any rate, here are some useful tidbits of information: Disneyland is 30 miles south of downtown L.A., right off I-5 in the city of Anaheim—you can see the Matterhorn from the freeway. The park is open daily; in summer, it remains open until midnight. Admission to the park, which includes all rides, costs around $80 per person per day, with discounts for extended visits; kids 9 and under save $6. For further park details, including operating hours, call Disneyland at 714/781-4565.

The major league baseball **Los Angeles Angels of Anaheim** play at Angel Stadium (2000 E. Gene Autry Way; 714/940-2000).

Disneyland opened in 1955, when there was nothing surrounding it; in intervening years, an entire metropolis has grown up around it. In 2001 the park was joined by the much smaller, more grown-up–oriented **California Adventure** theme park. Instead of cuddly cartoon characters, this billion-dollar park has thrill rides like California Screamin', a 55-mph roller coaster, and the excellent Soarin' Over California motion simulator, offering an airborne tour of the Golden State from Yosemite Falls to the Malibu beaches. California Adventure is separate from Disneyland, but a Park Hopper pass allows entry into both for $25 more than a one-park admission. California Adventure hours are shorter than Disneyland's, opening later in the summer and closing earlier year-round.

The whole Disney ensemble includes an upscale resort-hotel complex, surrounded by motels and yet more motels, and it is well worth staying overnight so you can get an early start, go "home" for a while, then come back for the nightly fireworks show. A highly recommended place to stay is the **Sheraton Park Hotel** ($129 and up; 1855 S. Harbor Blvd.; 714/750-1811), a block from Disneyland, offering spacious modern rooms (and a nice pool), with free shuttles every half hour to and from Disneyland.

Richard Nixon Presidential Library

If you've already done the Disneyland thing, or just want a foil to the empty-headed fun, there is one other Orange County attraction you really shouldn't miss: the **Richard Nixon Presidential Library** (daily; $9.95; 18001 Yorba Linda Blvd.; 714/983-9120), 10 miles northeast of Disneyland off Hwy-90. The library is

built on the very ground where the former president was born in 1913; it's also where he and his wife, Pat, are buried, side by side next to the restored Craftsman-style bungalow where Nixon grew up. No matter what your feelings toward him, the spare-no-expense displays do a fascinating job of putting his long career into the distorted perspective you'd expect from the only president ever forced to resign from office. Highlights are many, such as the pictures of the pumpkin patch where Whittaker Chambers concealed the microfilm that Nixon used to put Alger Hiss in prison as a Communist spy, next to photos of Nixon and JFK as chummy freshman U.S. senators sharing sleeping compartments on a train. The best-selling item in the gift shop? Photographs of Nixon greeting Elvis Presley, also available as mousepads, china cups, and fridge magnets.

Newport Beach

Back on the coast, if you want to get a sense of what wealthy Orange Countians do to enjoy themselves, spend some time along the clean white strands of **Newport Beach.** Located at the southern edge of Los Angeles's suburban sprawl, Newport started life in 1906 as an amusement park and beach resort at the southern end of the L.A. streetcar lines. Since then thousands of Angelenos have spent summer weekends at the **Balboa Pavilion,** at the southern tip of the slender Balboa peninsula, where the Fun Zone preserves a few remnants of the pre–video game amusements—a Ferris wheel, a merry-go-round, and those odd Pokerino games in which you win prizes by rolling rubber balls into a series of numbered holes.

Midway along the peninsula, near 23rd Street, Newport Pier is flanked by another holdout from the old days: the dory fleet. For more than a century small boats have set off from the beach here (often around midnight, landing back around 7 AM) to catch rock cod and more exotic fish, which are sold fresh off the boats at an outdoor market right on the sands.

A mile southeast of Balboa Pavilion, next to the breakwater at the very eastern end of Balboa peninsula, **The Wedge** is one of the world's most popular and challenging bodysurfing spots, with well-formed waves often twice as high as anywhere else on the coast.

To return to Hwy-1 from Balboa Peninsula, you can either backtrack around the harbor or ride the **Balboa Island Ferry,** which shuttles you and your car from the pavilion across the harbor past an amazing array of sailboats, power cruisers, and waterfront homes.

Crystal Cove State Park

Midway between Newport and Laguna Beaches, amidst the ever-encroaching Orange County sprawl, **Crystal Cove State Park** (daily dawn–dusk; $15 per car; 949/494-3539) protects one of Southern California's finest chunks of coastline. With three miles of sandy beaches and chaparral-covered bluff lined by well-marked walking trails, it's a fine place to enjoy the shoreline without the commercial trappings. Originally home to Native Americans, the land here was later part of Mission San Juan Capistrano and, until 1979 when the state bought it, the massive Irvine Ranch, which once covered most of Orange County.

The main parking area for Crystal Cove is at **Reef Point** near the south end of the park, where there are bathrooms and showers plus excellent tidepools, a fine beach, and a well-preserved collection of 1930–1950s beach cottages, where you can stay overnight ($33 and up; 800/444-7275). There is also a large section of the park inland from Hwy-1, through the oakland glade of **El Moro Canyon,** which gives a vivid sense of Orange County's rapidly vanishing natural landscape.

Laguna Beach

Compared with much of Orange County, **Laguna Beach** (pop. 24,100) is a relaxed and enjoyable place. Bookstores, cafés, and galleries reflect the town's beginnings as an artists' colony, but while the beach and downtown area are still very attractive, the surrounding hills have been covered by some of the world's ugliest tracts of "executive homes."

During the annual **Pageant of the Masters,** Laguna Beach residents recreate scenes from classical and modern art by forming living tableaux, standing still as statues in front of painted backdrops. Held every summer, it's a popular event and proceeds go to good causes, so get tickets ($15–112; 949/497-6582 or 800/487-3378) well in advance.

tableau from Laguna Beach's Pageant of the Masters

Right across Hwy-1 from the downtown shopping district, which is full of pleasant cafés and a wide range of art galleries, Laguna's main beach (called simply Main Beach) is still the town's main draw, with a boardwalk, some volleyball courts, and a guarded swimming beach with showers.

Many other fine but usually less crowded and quieter beaches are reachable from Cliff Drive, which winds north of downtown Laguna past cove after untouched cove; follow the signs reading Beach Access.

Laguna Beach has a number of nice places to eat; one place worth searching out is the small **Taco Loco** (640 S. Coast Hwy.; 949/497-1635), at the south end of the downtown strip, where the ultra-fresh Mexican food includes your choice of three or four different seafood tacos, from shark to swordfish, in daily-changing specials from about $2 each.

Places to stay are expensive, averaging around $150 a night, and include the beachfront **Laguna Riviera** (825 S. Coast Hwy.; 949/494-1196). At the top end of the scale, the newish **Montage** resort (30801 S. Coast Hwy.; 866/271-6953) has everything you could want from a hotel—all yours for $545 a day (and up!).

South of Laguna Beach, Hwy-1 follows the coast for a final few miles before joining up with the I-5 freeway for the 65-mile drive into San Diego.

San Juan Capistrano

Of the 21 missions along the California coast, **Mission San Juan Capistrano** (daily; $9; 949/234-1300) has been the most romanticized. When the movement to restore the missions and preserve California's Spanish colonial past was at its apogee in the late 1930s, its main theme tune was Leon René's "When the Swallows Come Back to Capistrano," popularizing the legend that these birds return from their winter migration every St. Joseph's Day, March 19. After wintering in Goya, Argentina, they do come back to Capistrano, along with several thousand tourists, but the swallows are just as likely to reappear a week before or a week after—whenever the weather warms up, really.

The mission, which has lovely, bougainvillea-filled gardens, stands at the center of the small, eponymously named town, a short detour inland along I-5 from the coast. Besides the birds, the main attractions include the small **chapel,** the last surviving church where the beatified Father Serra said mass, widely considered the oldest intact church and perhaps the oldest building of any kind in California, and the ruins of the massive **Great Stone Church,** a finely carved limestone structure that collapsed in an earthquake in 1812, just six years after its completion. Many

Mission San Juan Capistrano

visitors to the chapel are terminally ill patients saying prayers to St. Peregrine, the patron saint of cancer patients.

To get a sense of the huge scale of the Great Stone Church, a church patterned after the fallen building has been constructed behind the mission and now serves as the official mission church, open to visitors except during religious services. Across the street from this church, Mission Basilica, a Michael Graves–designed local **library** gives an intriguing postmodern take on the mission style.

The Coach House (33157 Camino Capistrano; 949/496-8930), two miles south of the mission, is one of Southern California's best small clubs for listening to live music.

San Clemente

At the southern tip of coastal Orange County, **San Clemente** marks the midway point between San Diego and Los Angeles. A sleepy beachside community, with frequent Amtrak train service and a nicely undulating stretch of old US-101 (El Camino Real) running through its heart, San Clemente is probably best known as the site of La Casa Pacifica, the one-time "Western White House" of former president Richard Nixon, who lived here following his election in 1968 and during his impeachment in the mid-1970s. The white-walled, mission-style house at the south end of Avenida del Presidente (the western frontage road to I-5) is more easily visible from the beach below, though the 25 acres of trees have grown up to obscure it in recent years.

Within a quick walk uphill from the handful of cafés and bars on and around the pier, **Beachcomber Motel** ($125 and up; 949/492-5457) is a tidy, old-fashioned motor-court motel, facing onto the open ocean. San Clemente also has burger place, **Duke's** (204 S. El Camino Real; 949/481-2040), in the mission-style downtown business district.

Old Mission San Luis Rey de Francia

In the sun-bleached hills above the blue Pacific, four miles east of the ocean off the I-5 along Hwy-76, **Old Mission San Luis Rey de Francia** (daily; $5) was the largest and among the most successful of the California missions. Its lands have been taken over by Camp Pendleton, and most of the outbuildings have disappeared, but the stately church at the heart of the complex survives in fine condition, worth a look for the blue-tinted dome atop the bell tower and for the haunting carved stone skull that looks down from the cemetery gate.

A long but worthwhile detour inland from San Luis Rey brings you to one of the least visited but perhaps most evocative of all the California missions, **Mission San Antonio de Pala** (sometimes closed Mon.; $2; 760/742-1600). Located on the Pala Indian Reservation, 20 miles east of San Luis Rey along Hwy-76, then another 100 yards north along a well-marked side road, Mission San Antonio de Pala is the only California mission still serving its original role of preaching to the native people, and it gives an unforgettable impression of what California's mission era might have been like.

Oceanside

At the southern edge of 125,000-acre Marine Corps Base Camp Pendleton, **Oceanside** (pop. 164,500) is one of the largest cities between Los Angeles and San Diego, but it offers little to attract the casual visitor—apart from a long fishing pier and guided tours of Camp Pendleton's amphibious-assault training exercises. But if you're in the mood to shop for camouflage gear, watch the muscle cars cruise Hill Street, get a $5 G.I. Joe haircut, or drink beer with a gang of young recruits, this is the right place.

The northwest corner of San Diego County is taken up by the U.S. Marines Corps's massive **Camp Pendleton** training base, which fills 125,000 acres, running for 17 miles along the coast and about 15 miles inland. Camp Pendleton (the base motto is "No Beach out of Reach") is the largest undeveloped section of the Southern California coast.

Oceanside is also home to one of the last survivors of the old, pre-Interstate, Coast Highway businesses: The **101 Café** (631 S. Coast Hwy.; 760/722-5220) has been open for classic road food since 1928; it often hosts classic car rallies and generally glows with neon-lit nostalgia.

South from Oceanside, all the way to San Diego, a very pleasant alternative to the often-clogged I-5 is the old alignment of US-101, now signed as County Road S21 (and occasionally, Coast Highway 101). Slower than the freeway but still in regular use, the old road is now the main drag of quaint beachfront towns like Carlsbad,

Leucadia, Encinitas, and Del Mar. If you have the time, it's a great drive, in sight of the ocean for most of the way.

Carlsbad: La Costa and Legoland

Named for the European spa town of Karlsbad, in Bohemia of what's now the Czech Republic, **Carlsbad** (pop. 105,328) was established in the 1880s as a spa town and vacation resort. A few remnants of the historic resort area still survive along old US-101 in the center of town. A few flower and strawberry fields surround the town, surviving against the ever-expanding tide of sprawl, and these days Carlsbad's spa-town heritage lives on at **La Costa Resort and Spa** ($249 and up; 760/438-9111), a 500-plus-room complex of luxurious rooms, health spas, golf courses, and tennis courts covering 400 acres of hills on the inland side of I-5.

> Some of the best views of the Southern California coastline can be had from the windows of the frequent Coaster commuter trains, which run right along the shore between Oceanside and downtown San Diego.

Carlsbad's other main attraction is the first American outpost of the popular European children's theme park **Legoland** (adults $69, children $59; 760/918-5346). Built out of millions of Lego bricks, and covering 128 acres above the Pacific Ocean, the park is divided up into multiple areas, including Miniland USA, where miniature landscapes modeled on New York, New Orleans, New England, and Southern California have all been constructed using more than 40 million of the trademark plastic bricks.

model of San Francisco made entirely from Lego blocks

South Carlsbad State Beach ($8 per car; 760/438-3143) three miles south of town, is one of the nicest and most popular places to camp on the Southern California coast, with its spacious campsites with hot showers ($35–50) spread out along a sandstone bluff above a broad beach. However, swimming can be dangerous because of strong riptides. If you don't want to camp or pay the parking fee, leave your car at the park

San Diego

Set along a huge Pacific Ocean harbor at the southwestern corner of the country just a few miles from the Mexican border, San Diego embodies the Southern California ideal. Around the turn of the 20th century, it rivaled Los Angeles as a boomtown based on wild real estate speculation, but while L.A. continued to expand by leaps and bounds, San Diego grew comparatively slowly. Instead of Hollywood glamour, San Diego's economy has long been based on the U.S. Navy, as evidenced by the massive former USS *Midway* moored right downtown. (San Diego successfully mixed its military and Hollywood influences in the movie *Top Gun*.) Despite a metropolitan population of more than 3 million people, San Diego still feels small and anything but urban.

The main things to see in San Diego are in **Balboa Park,** a lushly landscaped 1,200-acre spread on downtown's northeast edge, which was largely laid out and constructed as part of the 1915 Panama-California Exposition celebrating the completion of the Panama Canal. The many grand buildings, all built in gorgeous Spanish Revival style by architect Bertram Goodhue, have

Balboa Park

been preserved in marvelous condition and now house sundry museums, ranging from automobiles to fine art to a functioning replica of Shakespeare's Globe Theatre.

Balboa Park is also home to the **San Diego Zoo** (daily; $40; 619/231-1515), one of the largest and most popular in the world with over 4,000 animals kept in settings that simulate their natural habitats. You can see koalas

San Diego Zoo

and komodo dragons, panda bears and polar bears, plus gorillas, giraffes—you name it, if it's anywhere outside in the wild, it'll be here amidst the zoo's lushly landscaped 100 acres.

The **San Diego Padres** (619/795-5000) play at very popular, retro-modern Petco Park, right downtown in the Gaslamp Quarter.

Practicalities

The city of San Diego bends diagonally around its natural harbor, which makes orientation occasionally confusing. The main airport, Lindbergh Field, is on the waterfront just northwest of downtown—and has one of the swiftest final approaches of any urban American airport. Because it is small and relatively compact, San Diego is easy to get around. Downtown is walkable, and on a bike you could see most everything in a day. Buses operated by San Diego Transit (619/234-1060) fan out from downtown, while the light rail San Diego Trolley runs south from downtown to the Mexican border.

Though you may feel the need to duck when planes land at nearby Lindbergh Field, for breakfast try the **Hob Nob Hill** (2271 First Ave.; 619/239-8176), a classic 1940s coffee shop with great pecan waffles. For more all-American fare, head west to Ocean Beach, where **Hodad's,** a great old burger joint, awaits you (5010 Newport Ave.; 619/224-4623). San Diego's Old Town historic park holds some good old-school Mexican places, like the **Old Town Mexican Café** (2489 San Diego Ave.; 619/297-4330). In Balboa Park, soak up San Diego's Spanish Revival splendor while enjoying a meal at **The Prado** (619/557-9441) in the original House of Hospitality.

Places to stay are generally modern, clean, and comfortable, though rates vary with seasons (and conventions). For top-of-the-line accommodations, or just to appreciate the historic architecture, head to the wonderful old **Hotel del Coronado** ($299 and up; 1500 Orange Ave.; 619/435-6611), across the bridge from downtown on Coronado Island. Rising up in turreted glory, this fabulously grand Victorian-era resort hotel still caters, as it always has, to the four-star trade. It has been seen in many movies, including the great Peter O'Toole flick *The Stunt Man.* It's also where England's King Edward VIII is rumored to have first met the femme fatale who inspired him to give up his throne: Mrs. Wallis Simpson, whose first husband was first commanding officer of the local Navy base. The cheapest beds are at the **HI-San Diego Downtown Hostel** ($28 and up per person; 521 Market St.; 619/525-1531), in the historic downtown Gaslamp Quarter, or the hip **500 West Hotel** ($45 and up; 500 West Broadway; 619/234-5252), a boutique restoration of a 1920s YMCA. For more comfort and character, try **The Sofia Hotel,** a restored 1920s hotel ($135 and up; 150 W. Broadway; 800/826-0009). For surfer-friendly accommodations near Ocean Beach and Point Loma, try the **Ocean Villa Inn** ($99 and up; 5142 W. Point Loma Blvd.; 619/224-3481).

The best range of information is available from the **San Diego Convention & Visitors Bureau International Visitor Information Center** (1040 W. Broadway; 619/236-1212).

entrance, which is well marked on a surviving stretch of the old US-101 highway.

Del Mar and Torrey Pines State Natural Reserve

Most of the time, **Del Mar** (pop. 4,161) is a sleepy little upscale suburb of San Diego, with big houses backing onto more than two miles of fine beach. But in late summer, it comes to life for the thoroughbred racing season at beautiful **Del Mar Racetrack,**

A Torrey Pine, San Diego, Cal.—9

built by Hollywood types like Bing Crosby and seen in *The Grifters* and many other Hollywood movies and TV shows. The waves here are well suited to bodysurfing, but the sands can be hard to reach in summer because of a lack of parking—weekdays it's less of a problem.

South along the Camino Del Mar coast road from Del Mar, hang-gliders, tidepoolers, surfers, and beachcombers flock to the nearly 2,000 acres of bluffs and beaches protected in **Torrey Pines State Natural Reserve.** Named for the long-needled pines that grow naturally only here, the reserve is criss-crossed by hiking trails leading down steep ravines between the bluffs and the sands. Besides hang-gliders, Torrey Pines is prime air space for remote-controlled model gliders, which float gracefully in the nearly constant onshore breeze. The primary launching spot is the small city park at the south end of the reserve.

Overlooking the Pacific from atop a bluff at the south end of the reserve, the **Salk Institute** is one of the world's most important centers for research in the life sciences. Founded by the late Jonas Salk, designed by Louis Kahn, and modeled in part on the gardens of the Alhambra in Granada, the institute is open for **tours** Monday–Friday at noon (free; 858/453-4100).

Stretching inland and south from the Salk Institute, the hills are covered with faceless business parks around the spacious campus of **University of**

Pacific Beach, one of Southern California's better surfing spots, is home to the friendly, family-run **Paskowitz Surf Camp** (949/728-1000), held every summer since 1972.

California at San Diego (UCSD), beyond which spreads La Jolla and the greater San Diego area. On campus, learn all about local marine biology at the **Birch Aquarium** of UCSD's Scripps Institution of Oceanography ($14; 858/534-3474), from where you can amble along the shore to lovely La Jolla.

La Jolla

The wealthiest and most desirable part of San Diego, La Jolla sits along the coast northwest of the city proper, gazing out over azure coves to the endless Pacific. Besides the gorgeous scenery, great surfing (head to Windansea Beach for the best waves), beachcombing, and skin diving, a big draw here is the recently renovated **Museum of Con-temporary Art** (closed Wed.; $10; 700 Prospect St.; 858/454-3541), overlooking the ocean. Tons of good cafés and restaurants have long made La Jolla an all-around great day out, suiting all budgets—especially those with no upper limit.

At **Belmont Park** (3146 Mission Blvd.; 858/488-1549) west of Mission Bay, the Giant Dipper wooden roller coaster survives as the sole remnant of a 1920s beachfront amusement park.

Start the day off right at La Jolla's **The Cottage** (7702 Fay Ave.; 858/454-8409), where delicious food (including a divine buttermilk coffee cake) is served up on a sunny patio. For a memorable lunch or dinner, the very plush **Tapenade** (7612 Fay Ave.; 858/551-7500) is one of the best restaurants in Southern California, offering a deluxe mix of Mediterranean dishes. To continue the swaddled-in-luxury SoCal experience, stay the night at the elegant, Craftsman-style **The Lodge at Torrey Pines** ($350 and up; 11480 N. Torrey Pines Rd.; 858/453-4420), a modern re-creation of California's turn-of-the-20th-century Golden Age.

Driving San Diego

From La Jolla south, the US-101 highway is pretty well buried by the I-5 freeway. Old US-101 can still be followed, however, by following Pacific Highway past Mission Bay and Lindbergh Field toward San Diego Bay, where it becomes Harbor Drive—where the light rail San Diego Trolley now runs.

Index

A

abalone: 72
Aberdeen: 23
Adamson House: 122
Agness: 49
agriculture: Central Valley California 88; flower seeds 113
Albinger Archaeological Museum: 119
Alcatraz: 80
Alsea Bay Historic Interpretive Center: 41
amusement/theme parks: Balboa Pavilion 130; Belmont Park 139; Disneyland 127–129; Legoland 135; Santa Cruz Beach Boardwalk 87–88; Seaside boardwalk 31
Anaheim: 127
Anderson Valley: 69–70
Anderson Valley Brewing Company: 70
Andrew Molera State Park: 99
Año Nuevo State Reserve: 84–85
aquariums: Aquarium of the Pacific 126; Birch Aquarium 139; Feiro Marine Life Center 15; Monterey Bay Aquarium 90–91; Oregon Coast Aquarium 40
Arcata: 56–57
architecture: Adamson House 122; Balboa Park 136; Bottle Village 119; County Courthouse, Santa Barbara 116; Hearst Castle 105; Hotel del Coronado 137; Madonna Inn 109; Nitt Witt Ridge 106; Pacific County Courthouse 25; Port Gamble 10; Santa Barbara 116; Solvang 114
Art & Pumpkin Festival: 82
artichokes: 88
Asilomar Conference Grounds: 93
Astoria: 29–30
Astoria Column: 29
AT&T Pebble Beach National Pro-Am: 94
ATVs: 44
Avenue of the Giants: 63, 65

B

backpacking: 17, 100
Balboa Park: 136
Balboa Pavilion: 130
Bandon: 46–47
Bandon Driftwood Museum: 46
Bandon Dunes Golf Resort: 47
Bandon Historical Society Museum: 46
barbeque: 113
baseball: L.A. Dodgers 124; Los Angeles Angels 128; Portland Beavers 32; San Diego Padres 136; San Francisco Giants 81; Seattle Mariners 13
Battle Rock: 48
beaches: Cannon Beach 35; Carmel 95; Crystal Cove State Park 130; Garrapata State Park 98; Gaviota State Park 115; Guadalupe-Nipomo Dunes National Wildlife Refuge 112; Long Beach Peninsula 25–26; Newport Beach 130; Olympic National Park 21; Oswald West State Park 36; Pacific Coast Highway Beaches 120; Pescadero 83; Pfeiffer Beach 100; Point Lobos State Natural Reserve 98; Point Reyes National Seashore 76; Ruby Beach 21; Santa Cruz 86; "sleeper" waves 74; Sonoma Coast State Park 74; South Carlsbad State Beach 135; Sunset Bay State Park 46; Torrey Pines State Natural Reserve 138; Westport 24
Beard, James: 31
Belmont Park: 139
berries: 85
Big Basin Redwoods State Park: 85
Big Sur: 96
Big Sur Village: 99
The Birds: 74, 75
bird-watching: Bird Island 50; Leadbetter Point State Park 26; northern spotted owl 19, 40; peregrine falcons 107; Siletz Bay 39
Bixby Creek Bridge: 99

blowholes: 42, 68
Bodega: 74
Bodega Bay: 74–75
bodysurfing: 130
Bogachiel State Park: 20
Bohemian Grove: 72
Bolinas: 76–77
"Boontling" language: 70
Bottle Village: 119
Brookings: 50
Bubble Gum Alley: 109
Buellton: 114
Burns, Julia Pfeiffer: 102
butterflies: 93, 99

C

Cain, James M.: 121
California: 50–139
California Adventure: 128
Cambria: 106–107
Camp Pendleton: 135
Cannery Row: 90, 93
Cannon Beach: 35
Cape Arago State Park: 46
Cape Blanco: 47
Cape Disappointment: 27–28
Cape Flattery: 18
Cape Foulweather: 39
Cape Kiwanda: 38
Cape Lookout: 37
Cape Lookout State Park: 38
Cape Meares: 37
Cape Perpetua: 42
Carlsbad: 135
Carmel-by-the-Sea: 95
Carmel Mission: 110
Carson Mansion: 57
Castroville: 88
Cayucos: 107
cedar, Port Orford: 49
Channel Islands National Park: 118
Charleston: 46
cheese: 37
Cinerama Theatre: 13
Citizen Kane: 105
City Hall: 9
clamming: 25
Club Del Monte: 92
coastal walking: 74
Cobain, Kurt: 24
Columbia River: 30

Columbia River Maritime Museum:
  30
condor, California: 102
Confluence Project: 27
Confusion Hill: 65
Coos Bay: 45
covered bridges: 38
crab, Dungeness: 11
Crescent City: 52
cross-country skiing: 17
cruises: 118
Crystal Cove State Park: 130
Customs House: 90
cypress, Monterey: 98

D

Davenport Roadhouse at the Cash
  Store: 84
Dean, James: 107
Deetjen's Big Sur Inn: 102
Del Mar: 138
Del Norte Coast Redwoods State
  Park: 53
Depoe Bay: 39
Devil's Punchbowl: 39
diners: Apple Pan 125; Fog City
  Diner 81; Hi-Way 101 Diner 11;
  Louis', San Francisco 79; 101
  Café 135
Dipsea: 79
Discovery Trail: 27
Disneyland: 127–129
diving: Carmel 97; La Jolla 139; Salt
  Point State Park 72
Drift Creek Covered Bridge: 38
Drift Creek Wilderness: 40
Dune: 45
dunes, sand: Oregon: 44; Pismo
  Beach: 112
Dungeness: 14
Dutch community: 114
Dyerville Giant: 63

E

earthquakes: 60
Eastwood, Clint: 95
Ecola State Park: 34
El Camino Real: 110–111
elephant seals: 84–85, 105
Elk: 70
elk, Roosevelt: 20, 54

Enderts Beach Road: 53
Esalen Institute: 103
Eureka: 57–59
Experience Music Project: 12

F

farmers markets: 109
Feiro Marine Life Center: 15
Ferndale: 60–61
ferries: Balboa Island 130; Port Angeles to B.C., Canada 16; Seattle area 10
festivals: Art & Pumpkin Festival 82; AT&T Pebble Beach National Pro-Am 94; Irrigation Festival 11; Kinetic Grand Championship 58–59; Lavender Festival 11; Loggers PlayDay bash 23; Monterey Jazz Festival 90; Pageant of the Masters 131; Pebble Beach Concours d'Elegance 95; sand castle competition, Cannon Beach 35; Westport seafood 25
Fisherman's Wharf: 90
fishing: Astoria 29; Cape Kiwanda 38; Fort Bragg 66; Makah Indian Reservation 18; Moss Landing 88; salmon 24; Waldport 41
Fitzgerald Marine Reserve: 82
Flavel, George: 30
Flavel House Museum: 30
Florence: 43
folk art: Bottle Village 119; Nitt Witt Ridge 106; Romano Gabriel Wooden Sculpture Garden 57
Forks: 19–20
Forks Timber Museum: 20
Fort Bragg: 66–67
Fort Clatsop: 30
Fort Clatsop National Memorial: 30
Fort Point: 80
Fort Ross State Historic Park: 72–73
Fort Stevens: 30
Fort Worden: 9
49-Mile Drive: 79
Founder's Grove: 63
Friedlander, Lee: 24
fur-trapping outposts: 72

G

Gabriel, Romano: 57
Garberville: 64
gardens: Carmel Mission 97; County Courthouse, Santa Barbara 116; Esalen Institute 103; Golden Gate Park 80; Kruse Rhododendron State Natural Preserve 72; Mendocino Coast Botanical Gardens 67; Ramirez Canyon Park 121; San Juan Capistrano 132; Santa Barbara Mission 111; Sequim lavender 11; Shore Acres State Park 46
Garrapata State Park: 98–99
Gaviota State Park: 115
gay community: 73
Gearhart: 31
geologic formations: 35, 86
Getty Villa: 123
Giant Dipper: 87
Gold Beach: 48–49
Gold Bluffs Beach: 54
Golden Gate Bridge: 79
Golden Gate Park: 80
golf: 47, 94, 135
The Goonies: 28
Gorda: 104
Grays Harbor: 8, 23
Grays Harbor Historical Seaport: 23
Guadalupe: 113
Guadalupe-Nipomo Dunes National Wildlife Refuge: 112
Gualala: 71
Guerneville: 73

H

Half Moon Bay: 82–83
hang-gliding: 138
Harris Beach State Park: 50
Harte, Bret: 56
Haystack Rock: 35, 38
Hearst, William Randolph: 105
Hearst Castle: 104–106
Hearst family: 104
Heceta Head: 43
Henry Miller Memorial Library: 102
Highway 105: 24–25
Highway 112: 18
Higuera Street: 109

hiking: Andrew Molera State Park 99; Battle Rock 48; Big Basin Redwoods State Park 85; Cape Disappointment 27; Cape Perpetua 42; Fort Clatsop National Memorial 30; Jedediah Smith Redwoods State Park 51; Lake Crescent 17; Lake Quinault 22; La Purisima Mission 114; Lost Coast 61; Marin Headlands 79; Mount Olympus 21; Oregon Coast Trail 34; Oregon Dunes National Recreation Area 44; Oswald West State Park 36; Pfeiffer Big Sur State Park 100; Point Reyes National Seashore 76; Russian Gulch State Park 68; Salt Point State Park 72; Santa Monica Mountains Recreation Area 121–122; Torrey Pines State Natural Reserve 138
hippie enclaves: 64, 122
Hitchcock, Alfred: 74, 75
Hoh Rainforest: 20
Hollywood elite: 121
Hood Canal: 11
Hoopa Valley Indian Reservation: 53
Hoquiam: 22, 23
Hoquiam's Castle Bed & Breakfast: 23
horseback-riding: 99
horse racing: 138
Hotel del Coronado: 137
Hotel del Sol: 81
Humboldt Redwoods State Park: 62–64
Humbug Mountain State Park: 48
Huntington Beach: 127
Hurricane Ridge: 16

IJ
International Surfing Museum: 127
Jackson, Michael: 114
James Dean Memorial: 107
jazz: 90
Jedediah Smith Redwoods State Park: 51
Jeffers, Robinson: 97
Jenner: 73
Jessie M. Honeyman Memorial State Park: 44
J. Paul Getty Museum: 123

Juan de Fuca Strait: 18
Julia Pfeiffer Burns State Park: 103

KL
Kalaloch: 22
Kesey, Ken: 40
Kinetic Grand Championship: 58–59, 60
kite-surfing: 85
Klamath: 53
Kruse Rhododendron State Natural Preserve: 72
La Casa Pacifica: 133
La Costa: 135
Lady Bird Johnson Grove: 55
Lady Washington: 23
Laguna Beach: 131
La Jolla: 139
Lake Crescent: 16, 17
Lake Crescent Lodge: 17
Lake Quinault: 22
La Purisima Mission: 111, 114
lavender: 11
Leadbetter Point State Park: 26
Leggett: 64
Legoland: 135
Leo Carrillo State Park: 120
lesbian communities: 73
Lewis and Clark sites: Fort Clatsop National Memorial 30; Lewis and Clark Interpretive Center 27; Long Beach Peninsula 26; Seaside 31
lighthouses: Cape Disappointment 27; Heceta Head 43; Pigeon Point Lighthouse 83, 84; Point Arena 71; Point Sur 99; Tillamook Rock Lighthouse 34
Lincoln City: 38
literature: Miller, Henry 102; Steinbeck, John 93; Welles, Orson 105
Loggers PlayDay bash: 23
logging: Forks Timber Museum 20; Scotia 62; sustainable 25
Lompoc: 113
Long Beach: 26, 126
Long Beach Peninsula: 25–26
Los Angeles: 123–126
Los Angeles International Airport (LAX): 124

Lost Coast: 61
Lucia: 103

M
MacKerricher State Park: 66
Madonna Inn: 109
Makah Indian Reservation: 18
Makah Museum: 18
Malibu: 121–122
Malibu Colony: 121
Malibu Pier: 122
Mandarin Oriental: 81
Manzanita: 36
Marin County: 75
Marin Headlands: 78–79
maritime museums: 30
Marsh's Free Museum: 26
Marymere Falls: 17
Mateel Community Center: 64
Mavericks: 83
Mendocino: 68–69
Mendocino Coast Botanical
    Gardens: 67
Mendocino Headlands State Park: 68
military bases: Camp Pendleton
    135; Point Mugu 120
Miller, Henry: 102
missions, California: general
    discussion 110–111; Carmel 97;
    La Purisima Mission 114; Mission
    San Antonio de Padua 104, 110;
    Mission San Antonio de Pala
    134; Mission San Luis Obispo de
    Tolosa 108; Old Mission San Luis
    Rey de Francia 133; Old Mission
    Santa Inés 115; San Buenaventura
    118; San Juan Bautista 89–90; San
    Juan Capistrano 111, 132; Santa
    Barbara 117
Moby Dick Hotel and Oyster Farm:
    26
Monroe, Marilyn: 89
Montara: 82
Monterey: 90–92
Monterey Bay: 89
Monterey Bay Aquarium: 90–91
Monterey cypress: 98
Monterey Jazz Festival: 90
Monterey Peninsula: 91
Morro Bay: 107–108

Mo's: 41
Moss Landing: 88
mountain biking: Big Basin
    Redwoods State Park 85;
    Hurricane Ridge 17; inventors
    78; Lake Crescent 17; Marin
    Headlands 79; Point Reyes
    National Seashore 76
mountain lions: 21
Mount Olympus: 21
Mt. Emily: 49
Mt. Tamalpais: 77
Muir Woods: 77–78
Mulholland Drive: 124
Munson Creek Falls: 37
Museum of Contemporary Art: 139
Myers Flat: 63
Mystery Spot: 88

N
Nacimiento-Fergusson Road: 104
Nahcotta: 26
National Steinbeck Center: 93
Native American Reservations:
    Hoopa Valley Indian Reservation
    53; Makah Indian Reservation 18
Natural Bridges State Beach: 86
Neah Bay: 18
Neahkahnie Mountain: 36
Nehalem Bay State Park: 36
Nepenthe: 102
Netarts: 37
Neverland Ranch: 114
New Camaldoli Hermitage: 104
Newport: 40–41
Newport Beach: 129–130
Nitt Witt Ridge: 106
Nixon, Richard: 129, 133
North Head Lighthouse: 27
nude beaches: 100
Nye Beach: 41

O
Oaks Park: 32
Ocean Road State Natural Site: 42
Oceanside, California: 134–135
Oceanside, Oregon: 37
Odwalla: 84
old-growth forests: Del Norte Coast
    Redwoods State Park 53; Drift

Creek Wilderness 40; Humboldt Redwoods State Park 62; Jedediah Smith Redwoods State Park 51; Lake Quinault 22; Prairie Creek Redwoods State Park 54; Samuel H. Boardman State Scenic Corridor 49
Old Town Bandon: 46
Old Town Eureka: 57
Old Town Florence: 44
Olympic National Park: 8, 15, 19, 21
One Flew Over the Cuckoo's Nest: 40
Oregon: 28–50
Oregon Coast Trail: 34
Oregon Dunes National Recreation Area Visitors Center: 44
Orick: 55
Oswald West State Park: 36
Otter Crest Loop: 39
owl, spotted: 19, 40
oysters: Hood Canal 11; Nahcotta and Oysterville 26; Raymond 25; Seattle 13; Swan Oyster Depot 81; Tomales Bay 75; Yaquina Bay 40
Oysterville: 26

P

Pacifica: 82
Pacific County Courthouse: 25
Pacific Grove: 92–93
Pacific Lumber Company: 62
Pacific Way Bakery & Cafe: 31
Pageant of the Masters: 131
pampas grass: 104
Patrick's Point State Park: 55–56
Pebble Beach: 94
Pebble Beach Concours d'Elegance: 95
Pelican Bay State Prison: 52
Pepperdine University: 121
peregrine falcons: 107
Pescadero: 83
Petrolia: 61
Pfeiffer Beach: 100
Pfeiffer Big Sur State Park: 100
Piedras Blancas: 105
Pigeon Point Lighthouse: 83
Pike Place Market: 12
Pismo Beach: 112–113
plants, invasive: 104

Point Arena: 71
Point Dume State Beach: 120
Point Lobos State Natural Reserve: 98
Point Mugu: 120
Point Reyes: 75–76
Point Reyes National Seashore: 76
Polson Museum: 23
Port Angeles: 8, 12–14
Port Gamble: 10
Port Gamble Historic Museum: 10
Portland: 32
Portland Beavers: 32
Port Orford: 47–48
Port Townsend: 9–10
The Postman Always Rings Twice: 121
Post Ranch Inn: 101
Powell's Books: 32
Prairie Creek Redwoods State Park: 54
Prefontaine, Steve: 45
Prehistoric Gardens: 48
Presidio: 79
Princeton: 82
prisons: 52, 80
pumpkins: 82
Pygmy Forest: 69

QR

Queen Mary: 126
Quinault Loop Trail: 22
races, foot: 79
Ramirez Canyon Park: 121
Rancho del Cielo: 115
Raymond: 25
Reagan, Ronald: 115, 119
Redway: 64
Redwood National Park: 54–55
Reedsport: 44
Refugio State Beach: 115
Reggae on the River: 64
Return of the Jedi: 55
rhododendrons: 44, 67, 72
Richard Nixon Presidential Library: 129
roadside attractions: Anderson's Pea Soup 114; drive-thru trees 64–65; giant chessboard 108; Haystack Rock 36; old-growth redwoods 63; World's Largest Frying Pan 26; World's Largest Spruce Tree 22

Rockefeller Forest: 63
Rockport: 66
Rogue River: 49
Romano Gabriel Wooden Sculpture Garden: 57
Ronald Reagan Presidential Library: 119
Ruby Beach: 21
Running Fence: 75
Russian Gulch State Park: 68

S

sailboarding: 85
Salinas: 93
Salk Institute: 138
Salt Point State Park: 72
Samoa: 49–50
Samoa Cookhouse: 59
Sam's Grill: 81
Samuel H. Boardman State Scenic Corridor: 49
San Clemente: 133
San Diego: 136–137
San Diego Padres: 136
San Diego Zoo: 136
Sandland Adventures: 44
San Francisco: 80–81
San Francisco Giants: 81
San Francisco Solano: 110
San Francisco Zoo: 79
San Gabriel Arcángel: 111
San Juan Bautista: 89–90, 110
San Juan Capistrano: 111, 132
San Luis Obispo: 108–109, 112
San Miguel Arcángel: 111
San Simeon: 104
Santa Barbara: 111, 115–118
Santa Cruz: 85–86
Santa Maria: 113
Santa Monica Mountains Recreation Area: 121–122
Sappho: 18
Save the Redwoods League: 63
Scotia: 62
seafood: 12, 33; *see also* oysters
sea kayaking: 68, 108
Sea Lion Caves: 43
seals, elephant: 84–85
Sea Ranch: 71
Sears Fine Foods: 81
Seaside: 31

Seattle: 8, 12–13
Seattle Art Museum: 12
Seattle Center: 12
Seattle Central Library: 12
Sequim: 11
7 Cedars Casino: 11
17-Mile Drive: 94
Shelburne Inn: 26
Shelter Cove: 61
Shore Acres State Park: 45–46
Siletz Bay: 39
Simi Valley: 119–120
Siuslaw River Bridge: 43
sleeper waves: 74
Smith, Jedediah Strong: 51
Sol Duc River: 19
Solvang: 114
Sometimes a Great Notion: 40
Sonoma Coast State Park: 74
South Bend: 25
South Carlsbad State Beach: 135
spotted owl, northern: 19, 40
Stearns Wharf: 116
Steinbeck, John: 93
Stinson Beach: 76–77
St. Orres: 71
Stout Grove: 51
Strait of Juan de Fuca: 18
Sunset Bay State Park: 46
Sunset Boulevard: 124
surfing: bodysurfing the Wedge 130; Cape Kiwanda 38; Huntington Beach 127; La Jolla 139; Mavericks 83; Oswald West State Park 36; Pacific Beach 138; Paskowitz Surf Camp 138; Port Orford 48; Westport 25
Surfing Museum: 86
surf-kayaking: 25
Surfrider Beach: 122
Sutro Baths: 79
Swanton Berry Farm: 85

T

Tahkenitch Lake: 45
Tatoosh Island: 19
Theatricum Botanicum: 123
Three Capes Loop: 37
tidepools: Bolinas 76; Cape Perpetua 42; Half Moon Bay to Santa Cruz 83; Leo Carrillo State

Park 120; Lost Coast 61; Olympic Peninsula 15; Patrick's Point State Park 55; Torrey Pines State Natural Reserve 138
Tillamook: 36
Tillamook Air Museum: 37
Tillamook Cheese Factory: 37
Tillamook Head: 34
Tillamook Rock Lighthouse: 34
Tokeland: 24–25
Tomales Bay: 75
Topanga Canyon: 122
Torrey Pines State Natural Reserve: 138
Tourism Victoria: 16
Trees of Mystery: 53, 65
Trinidad: 56
Twilight saga: 20

UVWXYZ
Umpqua Dunes: 45
University of California: 86, 138–139
US-299: 56
Valley Ford: 75
Ventana Inn & Spa: 101
Ventana Wilderness: 100
Ventura: 118–119
Victoria, British Columbia: 16
Waddell Beach: 85
Waldport: 41
Washington: 8–28

waterfalls: Julia Pfeiffer Burns State Park 102; Munson Creek Falls 37; Pfeiffer Big Sur State Park 100; Santa Monica Mountains Recreation Area 121–122
Watsonville: 88
waves, sleeper: 74
weather: 16, 52
Wedge, The: 130
Welles, Orson: 105
Westport, California: 66
Westport, Oregon: 24–25
whale-watching: Cape Lookout 37; Garrapata State Park 98; Leo Carrillo State Park 120; Mendocino Coast Botanical Gardens 67; Ocean Road State Natural Site 42; Patrick's Point State Park 55; Point Lobos State Natural Reserve 98; Santa Barbara 117; Westport 24
wildflowers: 15, 53
wildlife viewing: Cape Lookout 37; elephant seals 84–85, 105; elk, Roosevelt 20, 54; Elkhorn Slough 89; Sea Lion Caves 43; seals 46; Tahkenitch Lake 45
Willapa Bay: 25
Willow Creek: 56
wineries: 69
World's Largest Spruce Tree: 22
World War II: 30
Yachats: 42

Photo and Illustration Credits

Ready to hit the open road?

Visit roadtripusa.com for trip ideas, maps, road trip routes, a Driver's Almanac of monthly trip suggestions, and more.

Web-exclusive features include Jamie Jensen's Road Tripper blog and free downloadable podcasts.

roadtripusa.com—the online source for road trippers!

www.moon.com

DESTINATIONS | ACTIVITIES | BLOGS | MAPS | BOOKS

MOON.COM is ready to help plan your next trip! Filled with fresh trip ideas and strategies, author interviews, informative travel blogs, a detailed map library, and descriptions of all the Moon guidebooks, Moon.com is all you need to get out and explore the world—or even places in your own backyard. While at Moon.com, sign up for our monthly e-newsletter for updates on new releases, travel tips, and expert advice from our on-the-go Moon authors. As always, when you travel with Moon, expect an experience that is uncommon and truly unique.

KEEP UP WITH MOON ON FACEBOOK AND TWITTER
JOIN THE MOON PHOTO GROUP ON FLICKR

ROAD TRIP USA
Pacific Coast Highway
2nd Edition

Jamie Jensen

Avalon Travel
a member of the Perseus Books Group
1700 Fourth Street
Berkeley, CA 94710, USA
www.avalontravelbooks.com

Editor: Kevin McLain
Fact checker: Haley Shapley
Copy Editor: Deana Shields
Graphics Coordinator: Domini Dragoone
Production Coordinator: Sean Bellows
Cover Designer: Domini Dragoone
Map Editor: Mike Morgenfeld
Cartographers: Mike Morgenfeld and Kaitlin Jaffe
Proofreader: Danielle Miller
Indexer: Rachel Kuhn

ISBN: 978-1-61238-187-9
ISSN: 1946-3278

Printing History
1st Edition — 2009
2nd Edition — June 2012
5 4 3 2 1